THE BIRDWATCHER'S GARDEN

THE BIRDWATCHER'S GARDEN

HAZEL JOHNSON
PAMELA JOHNSON

GUILD OF MASTER
CRAFTSMAN PUBLICATIONS

To Edward and Tony for all their help and encouragement

First published 2010 by
Guild of Master Craftsman Publications Ltd
166 High Street, Lewes, East Sussex BN7 1XU

This title has been created using material previously published in *The Birdwatcher's Garden* (first published 1999)

Reprinted 2011

ISBN 978–1–86108–870–3

A catalogue record of this book is available from the British Library.

Publisher: Jonathan Bailey
Production Manager: Jim Bulley
Managing Editor: Gerrie Purcell
Senior Project Editor: Dominique Page
Managing Art Editor: Gilda Pacitti
Design: Studio Ink

Colour origination: GMC Reprographics
Printed and bound in China by Hing Yip Printing Co. Ltd.

Previous page: Goldfinch.

Top right: Small flocks of redpoll are occasional winter visitors to gardens, sometimes joined by goldfinches and siskins.

Middle right: One of the most common garden birds, the blue tit readily comes to feeding stations.

Bottom right: Woodpigeons are becoming an increasingly common sight in gardens.

Contents

Top left: Gardens near woodland may encourage treecreepers to visit.
Middle left: Blue tits are found both in city and rural gardens.
Bottom left: The pheasant may feed below feeders and bird tables.

INTRODUCTION

This is a book is a guide for all who care about the environment and wish to help wildlife, particularly birds. It is for all gardeners who possess some form of garden – from a town windowbox or an allotment to a large rural acreage – and who are also interested in the birds around them. We have not included an identification key as there are many comprehensive guides available for reference in identifying birds.

Many bird populations are in serious decline; so much so that a number of species have been assigned to red (high alert) and orange (medium alert) lists by leading UK bird conservation organisations. Red listed birds that were common 25 years ago, including the skylark, tree sparrow, song thrush and spotted flycatcher, are now much reduced in numbers. In the latest review (2009), even the starling and house sparrow have joined the red list due to the loss of over 50 per cent of their breeding populations.

If you are interested in counting the birds visiting your garden, contact the British Trust for Ornithology (BTO) Garden Birdwatch: they run a survey for monitoring the numbers of birds using gardens. Keeping records of birds visiting the garden can be very illuminating and even more so if one joins the Survey. This will help them to monitor which birds are attracted into gardens and will give you access to the results in other gardens. The Royal Society for the Protection of Birds (RSPB) also monitors bird populations.

Changes in the countryside as a result of farming and woodland practices are occuring much faster than they used to, due to the increased mechanization of modern farming. Huge agricultural changes, road building and urban development have led to a disruption of the countryside. Mass monoculture, whether of imported forest trees or cereals, has taken the place of diversity. At the same time, hedges and wayside trees have been destroyed and woodland has become more fragmented.

Modern agricultural practices have also had an effect. The widespread use of chemical sprays, pesticides and herbicides has considerably altered the wildlife status and, along with the introduction of autumn- instead of spring-sown crops, this has resulted in the absence of insects and weeds in the fields during spring and summer and no spare cereals for bird consumption in the winter. Birds that find food from the edges of fields or set-aside land may suffer from a build-up of toxic chemicals in their bodies. These poisons can then be passed up the food chain, as happened in the 1960s; this led to a raptor decline. As we are at the top of the food chain, a healthy environment for birds would be a healthy one for us too!

Farmland birds could be threatened further by climate change, the pressures of increased food production, growth of the biofuel industry and the abandonment of set-aside land, where agricultural policy paid farmers to leave fields out of production. Large-scale cultivation of genetically modified crops, especially herbicide-tolerant and insect-resistant crops, such as maize, sugar beet and rape could have additional devastating effects on birds such as finches and buntings. Fields devoid of insects and weed seeds will not attract birds, so sympathetic gardens may become one of their last sanctuaries.

(Opposite) Blackbirds feed on fruits such as apples and pears.

There are many ways to make your garden appealing to birds. As long as it is sympathetic to their needs, they will enjoy to visit. Choose the right types of plant and try to provide trees and shrubs for them to use as observation posts, cover, shelter and roosting sites.

Attracting birds to the garden

WILDLIFE CORRIDORS AND GREEN NETWORKS

Wildlife tends to follow green passages of natural features when it needs to move from a particular district to find new territories. This can be for a variety of reasons, including an expansion in numbers, a need for more shelter, protection or food, and sometimes for a full or partial migration. Tree-lined rivers, canals and paths, disused railways, parkland and hedgerows – even road verges around a city – are all natural corridors along which wildlife can travel.

Natural corridors are frequently used by migrants and others to obtain access to isolated habitats. As our surroundings become even more congested and built up, the habitat 'islands' become smaller and many wildlife populations cannot survive without replacements from the outside; corridors and 'green networks' are needed to help link passages for wildlife. In the UK, natural corridors, designed as 'wildlife corridors', have been adopted by various local authorities, including London and other major cities. Some of these corridors penetrate into the heart of towns and cities, and should exclude any new building projects. They consist of green areas, whether these are made up of trees, parks or water, along which wildlife, including plants, can travel.

Illegal removal of plants has meant a scarcity of bluebell woods, which has upset the balance of nature.

CHEMICAL REACTION
||||||||||||||||||||||||||||||||||||||||||||||||||||||||||||||||||||||

Spraying with insecticides and herbicides has caused the loss of many flowers and insects, and led to birds becoming scarce in affected areas. If wildlife is unable to replace itself in a specified area, it will decline and disappear from there. If this phenomenon is widespread, it could eventually lead to the extinction of some species.

'Green networks' are defined as spaces within urban areas that are not built up or used intensively and join 'green' areas, including parks, playing fields and gardens. Together they can connect urban areas to suburban and rural landscapes. The huge area covered by suburban gardens, all of which play a part, is an obvious widespread network. Together, these green networks and corridors enable wildlife to reach at least some of the isolated habitat 'islands', especially within town centres.

If a corridor passes alongside a garden, the garden will benefit from the visitations of a greater diversity of wildlife. Some gardens can even act as source supplies, sending out replacements to other areas via the corridor or network of neighbouring gardens, parks and open spaces.

One disadvantage is that sometimes a corridor assists predators more than the species at risk, as predators seem to prefer the edges of habitats. Fortunately, all gardens, no matter how limited their resources, can assist in the movements of birds to safe havens.

The present trend in towns and cities is to improve the quality of life by enhancing the natural features. Making the most of the 'green' areas that are so important for wildlife also makes cities more pleasant for their human populations.

Many ponds have been lost or damaged but this one, situated in a conservation area, is a haven for wildlife as well as being enjoyed by local residents.

SYMPATHETIC GARDENING

Gardens are important, as they cover a vast area of ground throughout the country and can offer a valuable retreat or safe haven for many species. They are becoming even more important because of our changing climate.

Climate change will have a considerable impact on birds. Britain is predicted to have milder but wetter winters and hotter, drier summers with increasingly bad storms, floods and droughts. Warmer temperatures will induce many birds to start breeding earlier and cause changes to migratory behaviour. Large numbers of continental blackcap are already forgoing their long journeys to their overwintering grounds in Africa and are coming to Britain instead. If there are more long, hot, dry summers, it will impact on the breeding success of birds such as the blackbird that need a plentiful supply of earthworms and other soil-dwelling creatures to raise their brood. Alternatively, heavy rain during the breeding season causes a short supply of caterpillars. Blue tits had a disastrous year in 2007.

Attracting birds

How to attract birds into your garden is the first thing to consider. Gardens, however small, are potential nature reserves. Those in rural or suburban districts will appeal more to birds if they extend the habitat of the surrounding countryside, thereby offering refuge and food. Town gardens can enhance the neighbouring urban features and parks, becoming useful oases that will aid and boost the urban wildlife. A garden's geographical location, including its altitude, will influence which species visit, and the surrounding landscape should have a bearing on the composition of the garden. A garden planted in sympathy with its surrounding habitat will be attractive to the species that are most likely to be found in the area and this should increase the number of species that visit.

If you live in an agricultural area, it is much better to enhance your garden with hedges, and include more open spaces, as such an environment is appropriate for the species that are likely to be found there. Likewise, gardens with woodland in the area are best developed in sympathy with that woodland background. If there is heathland nearby, growing associated plants in your garden might encourage heathland birds to visit, possibly even some on the conservation danger lists, including skylark, whinchat and cirl bunting.

BIRD REQUIREMENTS

As a result of changes in the countryside, an increasing number of avian species now relies on gardens to provide the necessities of life. These include:

- Observation or singing posts
- Hedges and shrubs for shelter and roosting
- An open space for some species and a covered area for others
- Food and water
- Nest sites with nesting materials nearby
- Protection from predators for parents and fledglings

Many plants are multi-purpose, being used by birds to fill a number of these needs, though some gardens will not be large enough to provide for all of these requirements.

If you are developing a newly acquired plot of land, it is best not to uproot anything until you have assessed its potential value for birds. Most newly-planted trees and shrubs take at least several seasons to establish themselves and provide a reasonable amount of cover and food for birdlife. The amenities afforded by woody plants already present in the garden could be lost if they are replaced with new introductions, resulting in a loss of birds.

Garden composition

The shape, size and general structure of a garden is important. As far as possible, the greater the number of different plants growing happily in a plot, the greater the variety of wildlife that will be attracted to it. Whenever possible, it is highly desirable to have at least one tree, along with hedges, shrubs, herbaceous plants, some ground cover, a lawn and water. Water is vital for a bird garden whether provided in a drinking bowl, a pond or a stream.

Birds such as nuthatches can become frequent visitors to garden feeding stations.

Other elements that will attract and aid wildlife include the provision of additional bird food and nest boxes. (See Chapter 2, page 52 and Chapter 4, pages 100 and 116 for further information.)

A HEALTHY GARDEN

A garden cannot be left to run riot: not only will this annoy the neighbours, an unruly garden will not provide the best environment for wildlife. As all wildlife is interlinked, in order to help our diminishing birdlife our gardens need to be cultivated sensitively, with consideration for the natural scene. This will help to make them as healthy a place as possible not only for birds but for all wildlife.

Formal gardens

In a birdwatcher's garden, formal bedding is of limited value, as it can only be used by a small number of birds (robins, blackbirds and thrushes) to hunt for slugs, snails and earthworms. We have restricted our formal bedding to a narrow strip of land outside the front garden wall, and use it to experiment with different bedding schemes to find which attracts the most insects.

Bees and other insects benefit from plants with single flowers, such as evening primrose, honesty, mallow and garden cranesbill. Double flowers, which do not set seed, have no pollen, so fertilization cannot take place and insects are not attracted. Double flowers are usually formed by the alteration of the stamens into petal-like structures. If the plant is completely double, then all the pollen-bearing stamens will have been changed. Semi-double plants, including some cultivated primroses, may still possess some pollen and are able to set seed.

Flowers in the *Compositae* family (including daisies) have compound flowers that look double, but the 'outer petals' are really bracts surrounding small central florets, each of which is single.

Garden cranesbill *(Geranium endressii)*

Cowichan primrose *(Primula* group*)*

Daisy *(Bellis perennis)*

BIRDWATCHER'S TIP

||||||||||||||||||||||||||||||||||||||||||||||||||||||||||||||||||||||||||||||||||||||||||||||||||||

Plants that are grown from seed produce plenty of pollen, which attracts insects. An easy way to determine if a plant has pollen is to see if it can be grown from seed – in which case it may be listed in a seed catalogue.

Pest control

Most birds require large numbers of insects and other invertebrates, especially during the breeding season, so these 'pests' must not be eradicated if you want birds in your garden. Chemical sprays should be avoided, if possible, to maintain a healthy environment for wildlife: toxic chemicals are absorbed by the plants we eat, and birds are not attracted to gardens without insects. Similarly, when lawns are chemically treated earthworms are killed, the soil thus lacks aeration and the grass becomes unhealthy.

The best method of pest control is to remove infected material or to use a natural deterrent. Natural deterrents include pyrethrum and soft soap. Companion planting and biological controls can also be effective natural methods of pest control. (For more information, see Chapter 5, page 147.)

A discovery by the Royal Society for the Protection of Birds (RSPB) is that blackbird, song thrush and mistle thrush eggs are much thinner now than in the 1850s. This is due to a lack of calcium, which can also lead to low breeding success. The causes of calcium deficiency may be many, but lowering the toxic chemical level could help to lower the rate of decline of these birds.

CHILD-FRIENDLY GARDENS

There are hazards in nearly every garden. Small children need to be supervised and kept from eating any berries, fruits or other plant material as many are poisonous to some degree. Some plants which are poisonous to humans are not poisonous to birds. If small children frequently play in your garden, the best idea is to restrict fruits to those you know to be safe, such as blackberries, currants, loganberries, raspberries and strawberries.

A pond should also be delayed until the children have grown older. Drinking bowls for birds are fine and some children enjoy watching the birds bathe. The water must be kept clean in order to avert disease.

Elderberries (*Sambucus nigra*)

SUITABLE TREES

Trees are like beacons to some species of bird. Just as a ship is guided into harbour by lights, many birds fly from tree to tree, following the deepest cover. Trees are their arrival and departure points. The uppermost branches are often used as assembly points for flocks of such species as chaffinches, greenfinches, starlings and the winter migrants (bramblings, waxwings, redwings and fieldfares). These flocks will congregate in groups of all sizes, from small numbers right up to several hundreds or even thousands of birds.

Only a tiny proportion of birds are truly resident throughout the year; in the autumn months, and over winter especially, great flocks will rove around a district, or even further afield, in their daily search for shelter and food. It is not unusual for flocks of 100 or more tits, including blue, coal, great and long-tailed tits and perhaps a willow tit, accompanied by treecreepers and tiny goldcrests, to pass through some gardens in this way. It has been estimated that over 1,000 individual blue and great tits may visit a well-stocked garden at one time or other during the winter season.

Food sources

The choice of trees at a garden centre or nursery can be somewhat daunting. In a birdwatcher's garden, native trees are the most important, as they are host to innumerable numbers of insects. The two native oaks, English/common oak (*Quercus robur*) and sessile oak (*Quercus petraea*) are the best forest trees: 423 species of insect and mite are associated with them, including the caterpillars of moths, sawflies and the purple hairstreak butterfly as well as numerous aphids, beetles and bugs, together with their larvae. These, in turn, are preyed upon by numerous spiders, earwigs and lacewings. All provide an excellent food supply for many species of insectivorous bird. By contrast, the holm oak (*Quercus ilex*), a native of the Mediterranean that was introduced to Britain in the latter part of the sixteenth century, has only five associated species.

Other trees that attract an abundance of associated insects and mites include, in decreasing order: willow, silver/downy birch, hawthorn, poplar, Scots pine, blackthorn, common alder, elm, crab apple, hazel, beech, Norway spruce, ash and rowan. (See table on page 21.)

Common alder (*Alnus glutinosa*)

Hazel nuts (*Corylus avellana*)

Scots pine (*Pinus sylvestris*)

Blackthorn *(Prunus spinosa)*

Hawthorn/Quickthorn *(Cratagus monogyna)*

Silver birch *(Betula pendula)*

Further useful garden trees include fruit trees, particularly apple, pear, plum and cherry, wild cherry, fir, holly, plane, wild service tree and whitebeam. For smaller gardens, bird cherry, myrobalan cherry (cherry plum), Himalayan cotoneaster, field maple, black mulberry and common yew are appropriate, while in warmer, more sheltered regions the strawberry tree is one that will thrive.

Common hawthorn (*Crataegus monogyna*), often called quickthorn in nurseries and garden centres, is essentially a good hedging plant but can be grown as a small tree reaching a height of 35ft (10.5m). It produces a profusion of white flowers in late May/early June, followed by an abundance of bright red berries (haws) in the autumn. The smaller Midland thorn (*Crataegus laevigata*), which reaches a height of 15–20ft (4.5–6m), flowers some two weeks earlier. The pretty, double-flowering ornamental cherry trees should be avoided, as they do not set fruit. This deprives not only the birds, but also small mammals such as mice, voles and squirrels, of an essential autumn food supply. This is true for *Prunus avium* 'Plena', a white, double-flowering garden cultivar of the gean/wild cherry, which rarely sets fruit.

Hedges are extremely important: not only do they make excellent screens, they can also act as mini green corridors. (See table on page 22.) Planting a mixed hedge rather than a single-species hedge of privet or hawthorn is more beneficial to wildlife, as the different fruits will ripen at different times of the year, thus providing nourishment for birds over an extended period. More unusual hedging plants that can be included in mixed hedges are listed in the table on page 23.

Growth considerations

In selecting a tree, the size, height, shape and spread of canopy, and the amount of shade that it provides in high summer should all be considered. The lightly dappled shade from a silver birch would be preferable in a smaller garden to the deep dense shade of a beech.

Growth rate is another important consideration. For example, Leyland cypress (*Cupressocyparis leylandii*) is capable of growing 50ft (15m) or more in 20 years, whilst the common yew (*Taxus baccata*) may not even manage 16ft (5m) over the same period. Some forest trees take nearly a lifetime to reach maturity: beech may produce a first crop of mast after some 28 years but it usually takes anything up to 60 years.

The amount of light and shade in a garden depends on the type of tree that is planted.

Large forest trees, including ash, beech, lime, oak, poplar and sycamore, should only be planted in large gardens: their root systems cause damage if too near buildings and underground services. In a clay soil, take care in planting trees with strong, fibrous roots, particularly poplars and willows: the amount of water abstracted by their roots will cause the clay to crack. Ash trees are susceptible to 'elephant's foot' – a swelling at the base of the trunk that can lift paving and paths – and hence should not be planted too near any such features.

Climatic and geographic considerations

Choosing the right tree for a garden is also dependent on variables such as climatic conditions, latitude and altitude, sunshine levels, wind exposure and soil type. The tolerance levels of the tree may also be a significant factor. In coastal areas, at least some degree of salt-tolerance is required. A tolerance to air pollution is also an advantage, especially in industrial regions.

Coastal areas are particularly problematic, as plants must be able to withstand heavy buffeting by strong, salt-laden winds that can even batter a garden several miles inland. Shelter from the wind is important in any garden, but salty winds can severely damage non-marine plants, scorching young foliage and inhibiting healthy growth. However, with a good protective

BIRDWATCHER'S TIP

Oaks, beeches and other forest trees that are allowed to age naturally over the centuries become hollow inside and provide a much richer environment for birds and wildlife than newly planted trees. For this reason, if there are any well-established trees in your garden, they are worth preserving.

screen of trees and hedges against the prevailing wind, more fragile and less salt-tolerant plants can be grown, thereby increasing the diversity of plants in the garden. Trees with a relatively high salt tolerance include ash, hawthorn, common and holm oak, grey, Lombardy and white poplar, whitebeam and mountain ash. Sycamore may also be considered for large gardens. Although not a native tree, it does provide an abundance of aphids, which are a good food source for rare warblers, such as the tiny yellow-browed warbler, together with goldcrests, which are much more common, and occasional firecrests, which are sometimes found along the coast, having been blown off-route across the sea during their autumnal migration.

Young trees should be planted with stakes to support their growth and protect them from the elements.

Planting trees and shrubs

Deciduous trees and shrubs can be bought either as bare-rooted specimens (dug straight from the nursery soil), or as pot-grown plants. The latter can be planted at any time of year as long as the soil is not too dry, frozen or waterlogged. Bare-rooted specimens are best planted from mid-autumn to early spring, if the buds are still dormant, the weather is reasonable and the ground is not frozen. Evergreen trees and shrubs are often sold as 'root-balled' plants; these are best planted either in late September/early October or in April.

Bare-rooted plants that have been bought direct from the nursery need to be soaked in a bucket of water for at least an hour on arrival. If the planting conditions are unsuitable, these plants should be 'heeled in' the soil by digging a trench (unless the ground is completely frozen), and lying the plants in it in a single row, ensuring that their roots are covered with soil and that they are watered-in well.

To plant a tree or shrub it is essential to dig a hole slightly larger than the root spread size. Large trees generally need staking, especially on exposed sites. Place the stake in the hole first to avoid damaging the tree roots once the tree is in position. The tree should then be planted and the soil replaced with a mixture of topsoil and garden compost or well-rotted farmyard manure for added nutrients. Use sufficient soil to reach the same level as the old soil mark around the trunk or basal stem of the tree or shrub. Firm the soil around the base and water well. If necessary, water the hole before planting so that the soil is nice and moist but not waterlogged.

Newly planted evergreens and shrubs, especially before their roots have established, may need shelter and protection in winter from frosts and drying, icy winds that can cause their leaves to turn brown. Constructing netting windbreaks will help cut their exposure to these cold winds. Hessian sacking, loosely wrapped but securely tied around the plant, will give some frost protection, and inserting straw between the plant and the hessian will increase the insulation provided. If hessian isn't available, cloth material or windbreak netting can be used. New trees must not be allowed to dry out during their first year after planting, so especial care should be taken to water well during long, dry periods.

The method for planting a tree

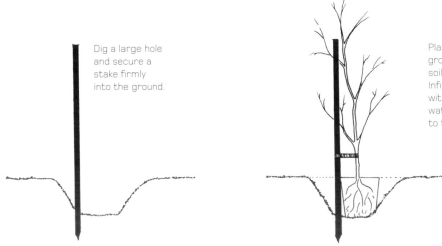

Dig a large hole and secure a stake firmly into the ground.

Plant the tree, ensuring that the ground soil level and the original soil level of the tree are equal. Infill the hole with soil enriched with garden compost. Firm and water-in well. Secure the tree to the stake.

TREES AND GROWING CONDITIONS

TREES	HEIGHT	GROWING CONDITIONS
Alder, common	60ft (19m)	Deciduous, thrives best in damp soils but not chalk. Sun or partial shade.
Ash	100ft (30m)	Deciduous, will thrive in most soils including chalk and clay.
Beech	100ft (30m)	Deciduous, thrives in most soils except clay and wet conditions.
Birch, silver	40–60ft+ (12–18m+)	Deciduous, thrives in most garden soils and good in exposed conditions.
Blackthorn	15–20ft (4.5–6m)	Deciduous, thrives in most soils and in exposed conditions.
Crab apple	30ft (9m)	Deciduous, thrives in most soils including chalk and clay. Tolerant of air pollution.
Elm	100–135ft (30–41m)	Deciduous, thrives in most soils but prone to Dutch elm disease.
Hawthorn	35ft (10.5m)	Deciduous, thrives in most soils including chalk and damp sites. Good in exposed and polluted areas.
Hazel	13–20ft (4–6m)	Deciduous, thrives in most soils and tolerant of exposed and polluted sites.
Norway spruce	120ft+ (36m+)	Evergreen, prefers acid soils, but will tolerate other conditions. Good in exposed sites.
Oak	100ft+ (30m+)	Deciduous, will thrive in any reasonable soils, including clays.
Poplar	50–100ft (15–30m)	Deciduous, thrives in most soils and suitable for exposed and polluted areas.
Rowan/Mountain ash	50ft (15m)	Deciduous, thrives in most soils and suitable for exposed and polluted areas.
Scots pine	120ft (36m)	Evergreen, thrives in most soils. Suitable for exposed areas but not tolerant of air pollution or shade.
Willow	35–80ft (10–25m)	Deciduous, thrives in damp conditions, tolerant of chalk and clay soils and of exposed and polluted areas.

HEDGES AND PLANTING CONDITIONS

	Deciduous (D)/Evergreen (E)	Native to Britain	Approximate planting distances (cm)	Approximate planting distances (in)	Planting conditions: Sun (S)/Partial shade (PS)	Any well-drained garden soil	Tolerant of chalk/alkaline soils	Tolerant of clay	Tolerant of damp/wet sites	Tolerant of exposed sites	Tolerant of air pollution
Alder	D	✓	60	24	S/PS	✓			✓		✓
Beech	D	✓	30–45	12–18	S/PS	✓	✓			✓	
Berberis	D		60	24	S/PS	✓	✓	✓		✓	✓
Blackthorn	D	✓	45	18	S	✓				✓	
Box	E	✓	20–40	8–16	S/PS	✓	✓	✓			
Cotoneaster	D + E		60–90	24–36	S/PS	✓	✓	✓		✓	✓
Gorse	E	✓	60	24	S	✓				✓	
Hawthorn	D	✓	20–40	8–16	S/PS	✓	✓	✓	✓	✓	✓
Hazel	D	✓	90	36	S/PS	✓		✓		✓	✓
Holly	E	✓	40–60	16–24	S/PS	✓	✓			✓	
Hornbeam	D	✓	30–45	12–18	S/PS	✓	✓	✓	✓	✓	✓
Laurel	E		40–60	16–24	PS	✓					
Lawson cypress	E		50–90	20–36	S/PS	✓	✓	✓		✓	
Leyland cypress	E		60	24	S/PS	✓	✓			✓	
Lonicera nitida	E		20–30	8–12	S	✓	✓	✓			
Privet	D	✓	30–40	12–16	S/PS	✓	✓			✓	✓
Pyracantha	E		60	24	S/PS	✓	✓	✓			
Sea buckthorn	D	✓	60	24	S/PS	✓			✓		
Snowberry	D		45	18	S/PS	✓	✓			✓	✓
Yew	E	✓	45	18	S/PS	✓	✓			✓	✓

OTHER USEFUL PLANTS FOR A MIXED HEDGE

Alder buckthorn

Amelanchier lamarckii

Buckthorn

Dogwood

Elder

Field maple

Plum myrobalan/cherry plum

Rose, dog

Rose, sweet briar

Spindle

Viburnum fragans

Viburnum tinus

Wayfaring tree

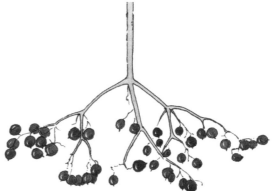

Elderberries *(Sambucus nigra)*

Spindle *(Euonymus europaeus)*

Wayfaring tree *(Viburnum lantana)*

Dog rose *(Rosa canina)*

June berry/Snowy mespilus
(Amelanchier lamarckii)

OBSERVATION POSTS

On arrival into a garden, birds need to know if there is any threat of danger, such as a stalking cat, and if there is food readily available. When a bird lands on an observation post, it can look around to determine whether there is any suitable shelter, any protection from predators and general interference, and if there are suitable feeding, roosting and breeding sites.

Generally, the taller the tree, the greater the cover it provides and the better it will be as an all-round lookout post. A mature Norway spruce (*Picea abies*) of about 115ft (35m) will attract crows, jackdaws, song and mistle thrushes, redwings, greenfinches and goldfinches to its uppermost branches, whilst woodpigeons, collared doves, blackbirds and robins often prefer vantage points further down the tree. Magpies, not such welcome garden visitors, are also attracted to the lower reaches of Norway spruce, especially in springtime, when they eye out nests in order to raid the eggs and young to feed their own broods.

Any plant or structure that is above the general surrounding foliage level, or even a lower one that provides a clear view, will be used by birds for various reasons. A crow will sit on top of an old electricity or telegraph pole to survey the activities of other birds in the neighbourhood, often with the view of finding food for itself or its young or for announcing its territorial claims. Jackdaws are similar: they will use vantage points on rooftops or on chimney stacks to observe potential food supplies and to spot danger or rivals in good time!

Swallows and house martins often avail themselves of electricity and telephone wires and other man-made structures near nest sites. The young birds, sometimes several family groups with adults nearby, will gather together to take a short practice flight. Later on, during migration, the numbers of birds build up, and any useful sites near nests are used as gathering posts.

Several years ago, before swallow numbers decreased, thousands of these birds used to pass through our garden each autumn. They would arrive in their hundreds from dawn onwards, sometimes accompanied by house martins, and would settle on any nearby wires, rooftops and even the top branches of the apple trees. On some days, group after group would arrive to swell the numbers again before another departure flight!

(Opposite) Overhead cable lines are an obvious stopping point for migrating birds to rest, or simply somewhere for birds to perch.

(Above) Swallows often perch on electricity and telephone wires close to their nesting sites.

(Left) Robins are a common sight in gardens and are very territorial, often perching on a familiar branch or post when they visit.

This series of events would be repeated every suitable morning and, to a lesser extent, in the evening. The garden became a busy main-line station for hirundines. However, a few years later the high numbers crashed and this area became, at best, a wayside halt. Unfortunately, the overhead electricity wires were replaced by an underground system, so there was no obvious stopping point for the migrating birds and they did not remain to feed on the many insects from the wooded banks of the river beyond the garden. Over the last year or two, it has become rare to see swallows around the garden. The two main contributing factors seem to be a shift in the inland migration routes, following the loss of the communal stopping point, and an overall decrease in the numbers of swallows. Like many species, swallows need both gathering and observation posts, for resting, observing and being observed by others joining the flight.

During migration, large swallow roosts often build up in reed beds, but it is unusual for these to be near gardens. If swallows are nesting in an old shed, garage or similar site, they will often perch nearby on a suitable ledge, high wall or rooftop and occasionally in nearby trees. Other swallows may then visit and join them at these sites, especially prior to or during migration periods.

Perches

Having somewhere to perch is equally important. Jackdaws spend hours sitting on the topmost twigs of tall trees like ash, oak and beech even in strong winds. Collared doves spend much of their lives in trees. When not feeding or nesting they can often be found sitting together on a favourite branch dozing, sleeping, preening or performing ritual amorous advances. One pair of collared doves in our garden habitually enact their courtship on the branch of an old apple tree just outside our kitchen window.

SHELTER AND PROTECTION

A sheltered garden is a more attractive place to birds and wildlife than an unsheltered one, and it also has many other distinct advantages. In exposed sites the wind can cause damage, ranging from snapping top-heavy blooms and flattening whole flowerbeds, to breaking off branches and even uprooting trees. Wind can distort the growth of trees and cold, drying winds will even scorch evergreens. Exposed sites are cold sites. When the winter wind blows, the wind chill factor exacerbates the coldness, making it feel several degrees cooler than it actually is. Large towns and cities are generally considered to be more sheltered and warmer during the winter than the surrounding countryside. It has been estimated that the temperature in the city and country may vary by 1–3°F (0.5–1.5°C) and up to 10°F (5°C) on still nights. This difference has usually levelled by morning, but the overnight temperature could mean the difference between life and death. L. A. Batten's comparison of the survival rate of blackbirds (1973) showed a higher rate of survival in the warmer, more sheltered town and suburban gardens than in the surrounding countryside. During particularly harsh weather conditions in winter, many more unusual birds – siskins, waxwings, redwings and fieldfares – will come into the garden looking for shelter and food.

The effect of solid structures and plant barriers on wind turbulence.

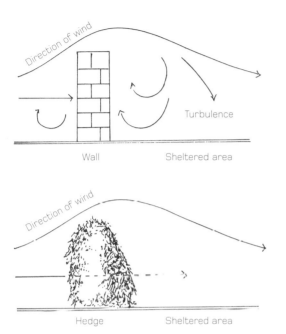

Living plant barriers, such as rows of trees or hedges, make excellent windbreaks. These are better than solid structures like walls and fencing because they filter the wind, reducing its speed, strength and damaging ferocity, and provide some shelter on the leeward side. Birds need sheltered places, especially during gales, in order to feed without being battered and ruffled by blasts of wind.

When wind hits solid structures it results in wind turbulence, causing strong swirling eddies that can damage plants on either side of the wall. Under these conditions a small bird would have great difficulty in reaching cover quickly if danger threatened.

With plant barriers, the taller it is, the greater the sheltered area provided on the leeward side – sometimes as much as 15 to 20 times the height of the barrier, depending on the force of wind and the type of plant. (See illustration top left.)

Suitable trees

Trees that are suitable for windbreaks in larger gardens include the following: Lawson cypress, small-leaved lime, Norway spruce, holm oak, poplars (aspen, grey, Lombardy and white), rowan/mountain ash, sycamore, whitebeam and white willow. Good hedging plants include beech, blackthorn, cotoneaster, hawthorn, hornbeam, privet and sea buckthorn.

(Opposite) Blackthorn in flower is very attractive to early butterflies and other insects. It is also a good shelter and nesting plant.

SHELTER IN COASTAL GARDENS

In coastal gardens, shelter is particularly important, as the strong salt winds are problematic: many plants cannot tolerate salty conditions. Sea buckthorn (*Hippophae rhamnoides*) is an ideal hedging plant under these conditions. However, it is dioecious and thus both male and female plants are necessary (in a ratio of one male to three female) if the flowers are to be pollinated and the orange berries produced. These berries ripen in the autumn. Other shrubs and hedging plants suitable for coastal gardens include *Cotoneaster lacteus*, *Elaeagnus*, *Euonymus japonicus*, gorse, hawthorn, holly (*Ilex aquifolium*), *Pyracantha*, tamarisk and *Viburnum tinus*.

Cover

Another essential for a bird garden is cover; a place to fly to in times of danger that will keep small birds out of sight and safe from harm. This may be provided by trees, large bushes, thick hedges, shrubs or low-lying ground-cover plants, depending on the bird. Sparrowhawks, kestrels and, at night, tawny owls may take their toll on birds even in suburban gardens. A female sparrowhawk is capable of taking a bird as large as a woodpigeon. An even greater threat to garden birds comes from that lovable human companion, the cat, whose wild instincts make it such an effective killer. Another cause of death, especially of blackbirds in built-up areas, is traffic. Blackbirds have a tendency to fly low and skim across roads to visit neighbouring gardens; they court death every time.

Large, brown, female sparrowhawks are becoming a more common sight in suburban gardens, though the blue-grey male, a smaller, shyer bird, is less likely to be seen, as they are more inclined to hunt in woodland. They are fascinating birds to watch, with their breathtaking and dynamic aerial agility, ferocious, bright yellow talons and menacing, yellow eyes. One particular female in our garden crash-landed, after an unsuccessful swoop, on the top of a thick cotoneaster, *Lonicera nitida* and quince hedge and proceeded to bounce up and down, flapping her wings fitfully, using the hedge like a trampoline in an effort to flush out the seven or eight house sparrows that were deep inside.

(Top right) *Pyracantha* growing against a wall provides good nesting, cover and berries for thrushes and greenfinches.

(Right) The sparrowhawk's prey is mainly birds. Garden birds need places to hide from such predators.

TIMID BIRDS

Some birds are more timid and shy than others and will not come into gardens if there is a disturbance and no cover. Woodland birds, including great spotted woodpeckers, nuthatches and treecreepers, like the cover of trees.

This wren, along with dunnocks and song thrushes like the cover of hedgerows and the edges of borders. All manner of small mammals also like this cover, including bank voles, shrews and mice.

Every now and again she swooped to ground level, first on one side and then the other, before returning to the top of the hedge for more 'bouncing'. This continued for several minutes before she gave up and flew off. As long as the sparrows remained deep in the cover of the hedge, she was unable to reach them.

A low wall in the front garden, in order to screen off a busy road, together with a few shrubs, may provide enough cover to encourage song thrushes, blackbirds, robins, blue tits, wrens and dunnocks to visit and even lead to a few surprises, such as a weasel passing through.

ROOSTING SITES

A good roosting site is one that provides the greatest cover, shelter and protection from the cold and from predators. The more sheltered a site the birds can find, the better their chances of survival, especially through severe winter weather. Roosting birds lose body weight overnight as a result of the energy used to maintain their body temperature, so any site that is a few degrees warmer than its surroundings will give the birds a distinct advantage. (See table on page 33.)

Some birds roost communally; long-tailed tits may be found in family groups, huddled closely together in a line on a twig inside a thick hedgerow. The dominant birds take central position leaving the weaker birds at the ends more likely to die off in cold conditions.

Starlings might fly anything from a few miles to over 20 miles (5–34km) from their feeding grounds to their roost in the evening. They often roost in large cities and towns where they arrive in their hundreds and thousands, their numbers inflated by an influx of overwintering birds from the continent. The famous roost on the pier at Brighton has as many as 40,000 birds in December. Starlings arrive to roost, squabbling and chattering on building ledges, TV aerials, chimney pots – every possible site – taking full advantage of the artificial heat and safer environment of the city. Many large roosts, both in towns and in the country, used to house over a million birds, but even the starling is now in decline and many major city roosts have disappeared. Other species roost alone. While the female great spotted woodpecker stays overnight in her nest hole, the male may excavate another hole nearby. Treecreepers, sometimes in family groups, roost in clefts or behind the bark of trees and show a particular preference for roosting in wellingtonias. (This giant redwood is a tree too large for the average garden!)

In general, in rural areas, roosts of finches, starlings and thrushes (including blackbirds, song thrushes and the winter migrants – redwings and fieldfares) are usually located in thick, shrubby vegetation, though starlings will also roost in a stand of trees. This vegetation includes thick hawthorn hedges or evergreens such as laurel, rhododendron and holly. In our garden during winter, up to seven blackbirds regularly roost in an overgrown patch of snowberry, behind our neighbour's summerhouse, next to a spotted laurel, beneath a tall, ivy-clad Norway spruce. Frequently joining the blackbirds in this sheltered spot are dunnocks and chaffinches. Collared doves roost together overnight on a single branch in the *Prunus* tree, as evidenced by a conspicuous pile of droppings on the lawn beneath.

(Left) Evergreen *Virburnum tinus* provides a sheltered roosting site for birds.

(Opposite) A starling is a common garden visitors, but often roosts communally.

(Above) The treecreeper is an active bird,
which lives in trees and can often be found
roosting in cracks or behind the bark.

Ivy is also an important roosting site, as it grows
up walls and scrambles among old mature trees.
It provides shelter not only for birds, including
house sparrows, pied wagtails, blue tits, wrens,
starlings and greenfinches, but for insects too.
Butterflies in particular are fond of hibernating
on ivy-clad walls.

ADVENTUROUS ROOSTING

Some birds are great opportunists and will roost in the
oddest places. House sparrows have been known to
roost in street lamps, in thatch, and under the eaves
of buildings, and are ready to exploit old house martin
nests and holes in masonry. In rural districts they
are often found in tall hedgerows in association with
greenfinches and yellowhammers.

Some birds, such as blue tits, great tits, nuthatches and
wrens, will roost in man-made nest boxes. Wrens have
been known to creep into garden sheds and greenhouses
and roost overnight amongst the flowerpots.

GARDEN BIRDS AND THEIR ROOSTING SITES

	Holes, hollows and crevices in trees	Mature deciduous trees	Conifers	Large evergreen trees and shrubs	Tall, thick hedgerows	Bushy shrubs	Creepers/climbing plants	Building ledges and roofs	Eaves and holes in masonry	Thatch	Nest boxes	Thick ivy cover
Sparrowhawk		✓			✓							
Woodpigeon				✓								
Collared dove		✓	✓									
Tawny owl	✓	✓									✓	✓
Great spotted woodpecker	✓											
Pied wagtail				✓		✓		✓			✓	✓
Wren	✓				✓						✓	✓
Dunnock				✓	✓	✓						
Robin					✓	✓					✓	
Blackbird				✓	✓	✓	✓					✓
Song thrush				✓	✓	✓						
Goldcrest			✓									
Long-tailed tit	✓	✓	✓		✓	✓						
Coal tit	✓	✓	✓		✓					✓	✓	
Blue tit	✓			✓	✓				✓	✓	✓	✓
Great tit	✓	✓							✓	✓	✓	
Nuthatch	✓										✓	
Magpie		✓	✓		✓							
Jackdaw		✓	✓					✓				
Starling	✓		✓	✓				✓	✓		✓	
House sparrow		✓		✓	✓	✓	✓		✓	✓	✓	✓
Chaffinch		✓		✓	✓	✓						
Greenfinch				✓	✓	✓						
Goldfinch		✓			✓	✓						

It is a joy to watch birds visit your garden, but it's even better if they really utilize it! You can encourage them to feed and nest in your garden if you are aware of their feeding habits and provide them with recommended food plants, song posts, nest sites and nest materials.

Breeding and feeding

BREEDING HABITS

There are plenty of hazards for birds to overcome during a breeding season without additional disturbance by humans, whose actions can upset the balance of nature and cause the loss of species. There were an estimated 3,000 million passenger pigeons in the United States, until men started hunting them excessively during the late nineteenth century. Snow and Perrins (1998) state that the population had crashed by 1870 and now passenger pigeons are extinct.

The robin finds a prominent position in the garden and uses it as a song post.

Song posts and territorial markers

When birds first arrive in a garden, many use a tree or some other prominent position as an observation post. If they stay, they continue to use it as a song post, and sometimes as a territorial marker, during the breeding season. Singing can both attract a mate and indicate the boundaries of an individual's territory, with several singing posts marking out the size and shape of the bird's stake. The size of the territory marked depends on the species and on the individual; larger areas are necessary if food and shelter are in short supply.

Singing from a number of positions helps to increase a male's chances of procuring a mate. Also, in some species, the female prefers the best singer: the one with the best repertoire or the loudest and longest song. These differences seem to indicate to the female which is the healthiest bird and thus the best mate for producing strong, healthy offspring.

Blackbirds are quite adaptable in what they will use as a song post – a tall shrub, a tree with a view, a rooftop and the edge of a wall may all be adopted. This is true of many of the more common birds, although some prefer cover from which to sing so that they can advertise their presence in relative safety.

Telephone wires are greatly favoured by swallows, especially when they are positioned near a nest site, but trees, shrubs and undergrowth, almost anything, can be used for song and territorial purposes.

If the territory of a bird is so large that it cannot keep a watch over it all, a different strategy may be used. Woodpeckers need a very large area in order to locate enough food. To indicate what is their territory, they use a variety of signals. Green woodpeckers make resonant calls that echo throughout their woodland habitat, while the great spotted woodpecker will drum loudly on dead wood, even an old wooden telephone or electricity pole. This sound carries a long way. Woodpeckers will also mark their favourite trees by bark stripping, leaving shreds of bark strewn on the ground below.

At the beginning of the breeding season, a great spotted woodpecker used to drum on a wooden electricity pole near us, early in the morning. The sound from his 'singing post' carried extremely well! Another great spotted woodpecker in our garden used to shred the bark, not just to find insects but also to mark his territory, on a tree stump used to support a bird table!

Nest sites

Most birds commence breeding after the male has established a territory with song posts and attracted a mate. Then, either the male, the female or both birds will seek out a nest site, which need not be in the centre of a demarked area. However, finches that feed their nestlings on insects – greenfinches, goldfinches, linnets,

TERRITORIAL DISPUTES

Males will defend their territory against intruders of the same species and against a predator. When there is an intruder, or when the territories of two male birds overlap, especially early in the breeding season, this can cause aggression. Blackbirds are easy to watch, as they frequently give call notes, semi-alarms or even a jumbled mutter of a song as they try to establish their rights. Sometimes a dispute is carried out from tree to tree or tree to bush, but often the scene takes place on a lawn. Two males will hop backwards and forwards continuously with one bird trying to edge the other either further up or down the lawn. One may even rush at its opponent, resulting in many noisy squawks and squabbles. These manoeuvres may last some time and be repeated on many successive days before one bird gives up and flies away. Not only territory is sought; the other bird's mate may also be desirable to the intruder!

siskins, redpolls and serins – pair off whilst still in the winter flock. After pairing, the female finds a nest site around which the male will then establish a small territory. Feeding still takes place mainly in the flock, outside the territory.

Blackbirds usually start to lay their eggs in March, but with the changing climate and increasingly mild winters, egg-laying often begins much earlier.

Large trees

Birds that nest in large trees, often forest trees, include sparrowhawks and corvids. It is common for a carrion crow to nest 60ft (20m) or more up in the forked branches of beech, elm, sycamore or other large, mature trees. Jays will nest in birch, whereas magpies frequently choose lower nest sites, often in hedgerow trees. Some small passerines will nest in forest trees. However, most trees of this size are only practical in very large gardens. (See table on page 45.)

Nesting in holes

Some hole-nesting species, like woodpeckers, require mature trees with rotten wood in order to excavate a nest. Occasionally, the lesser spotted woodpecker – the smallest – will use old,

The tawny owl typically nests in a hole in a tree.

decaying trees in an orchard. If the tree diameter is large enough, green woodpeckers can also avail themselves of these sites.

Other holes in the orchard trees will be utilized by the adaptable tits. Great tits frequently take over sites from blue and coal tits. The latter cannot compete for nest sites with either of the two heavier tits, so they frequently resort to mouse holes at the base of trees if they are unable to find anything more suitable. Other large hole users are owls; in the south of the UK, little owls will nest in old orchards. Stock doves, nuthatches and treecreepers are also hole nesters. Treecreepers frequently site their nest behind cracks in the bark.

A conifer, of medium proportions, can easily become the nest site for collared doves, goldcrests and various finches, including the occasional redpoll or siskin, though these usually prefer a more forest-like environment. Some established gardens have extensive shrubberies or wooded hedgerows. If these are in a rural setting, there is a possibility that nesting birds could include partridge, pheasant, woodcock and green woodpecker.

Hedges, trees and bushes

As most gardens have room for only one or two small trees, hedges, ornamental shrubs and climbers are invaluable. A monoculture hedge (a hedge planted with only one species) has only limited value compared with a hedge comprising several different species. Monoculture hedges can be 'improved' by the addition of shrubs and by planting small trees and herbaceous cover in front of them. These bushes act as distinguishing features, demarking various points along the hedge. Birds nesting in a hedge need these features to be able to locate their nest site readily and speedily, especially in emergencies. Hawthorn and blackthorn, members of the

Snowberry (*Symphoricarpos rivularis*)

Rosaceae family, can be grown as trees, but for nesting birds they are much more valuable as shrubs or in a hedge. Their thorny stems offer protection against predators and many birds are known to breed in them. Other useful trees and hedging shrubs include elder, cotoneaster, *Berberis*, *Lonicera nitida*, beech, box and the invasive snowberry, especially when ivy-covered. (Examples are listed in the table on page 46.)

Early nesters prefer evergreen trees, hedges and shrubs because when they start to nest, these provide better cover. Deciduous hedges and shrubs are used more later in the season, once they have come into leaf.

For nesting at a lower level, herbaceous and border plants, vegetables, general ground cover and the bases of overgrown hedges provide excellent nest sites.

Ivy clambering over tree stumps and banks is much appreciated by robins, wrens and blackbirds. (See table on page 47.)

A hawthorn tree, with its highly-prized berries, can be used as an observation post and a nesting area protected by thorns.

BIRDWATCHER'S TIP
||||||||||||||||||||||||||||||||||||||||||||||||||||||||||||||||||||||||||||||||||||||||

Berberis, Pyracantha and other thorny, predator-resistant hedges and shrubs should be handled with caution, as they can cause allergic reactions in some people.

Thick hedges are a favourite nest site for many birds.

UNDISTURBED NEST SITES

Quiet, untidy corners with a nettle, bramble, briar, bracken or fern patch are possible nest sites for some warblers; the willow warbler, which likes grassy banks, hardly ever nests within 165ft (50m) of a main road because of traffic noise.

Shrubs and climbers

Shrubs and climbing plants that are growing against buildings, house walls, sheds and so on, are other favoured nest sites. If there are ledges behind or within the climber, whether it be ivy, **clematis**, Russian vine, Virginia creeper, wisteria or another creeper, they can be used not only by the usual blackbirds, song thrushes and greenfinches, but also by spotted flycatchers, long-tailed

Bramble thickets provide an excellent nesting site and food for birds.

Old man's beard, *Clematis vitalba*, is a fast-growing climber, seen here clambering over an old apple tree.

(Right) Russian vine, *Fallopia baldschuanica*, provides excellent cover.

tits and pied wagtails. One of the most notable early records of such a new site was of a black redstart in Durham City, nesting in a cherry tree growing up against an old, weathered sandstone garden wall. The branches and weathered stones together made a perfect ledge for the nest, which held four eggs. Unfortunately, this was in Victorian times and to prove the existence of a scarce bird nesting, both eggs and nest were collected and the birds were shot. The nest was lost after being in a museum for some time and the cherry tree has since been removed. Nowadays, to examine or photograph a rare bird's

breeding site anywhere requires a licence, so if anything unusual does appear to be nesting, contact one of the major wildlife or ornithological organizations for advice on how to proceed. (For useful addresses, see Sources of Information on page 170.)

Nest materials

Nests vary from the very large structures built by such birds as corvids and raptors, to the tiny, inconspicuous nests of goldcrests, so the materials used differ considerably. The composition of a nest of a single species can be affected by both the site chosen and the availability of suitable materials and is often highly variable. If an essential component is missing, birds will seek new territories, and if that option is not open, they may not breed that season. Finding and establishing new territories is difficult. With many species, quite a large percentage of birds, especially young, first-time breeders, do not manage to establish a territory and so are unable to breed. The commoner birds are more adaptable with regard to nest materials and will utilize almost anything that appears handy, including plastic, string, foil and paper. A marsh tit seized on the dusty dog hairs that had escaped out of a hoover bag on a windy day. This obviously gives them a major advantage over those species with more stringent nesting requirements.

The majority of nests found in gardens have a foundation and general structure made from relatively coarse ingredients (see tables on pages 48 and 49), with a softer, often warmer, inner lining suitable for the incubation and rearing of chicks. Some birds use nests left from previous seasons as the foundation for their new nest. A few birds, often individuals, like to select an external ornamentation or rim decoration. The former frequently camouflages the nest, but the latter just seems to please the individual and frequently renders the nest more conspicuous. Flower petals and old honesty seed heads do nothing to conceal a nest!

Some birds are quite fastidious, if they have a choice. We watched a carrion crow collecting nest materials. It gathered some forest tree twigs, but also snapped off twigs from a Worcester Permain apple tree, even though there were several other varieties present. Each year, in our garden, jackdaws spend considerable time trying to undo the strands of twine or string that we use to tie our roses to a trellis. This year, jackdaws from different nests repeatedly attacked an old apple tree in order to strip its bark. One bird only collected bark from the ultimate twigs, one from medium-sized twigs and a third from thick boughs! (See tables on pages 50 and 51.)

Nest materials may be gathered over an extended period in the early spring. This seems to depend to a large extent on the vagaries of the weather. If it is unfavourable, the nest may take weeks to complete, and it may then still be left for some time without any egg laying. Later in the season repeat nests, necessary because of failures or second broods, are usually built in a hurry, the preparation time being reduced to a few days, or even one day, before egg laying.

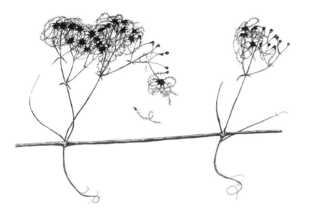

Traveller's joy, also known as old man's beard, (*Clematis vitalba*) seed heads are often used in nest building.

Influences on breeding

Various factors affect the breeding success rate of birds. For many species the percentage of failed nests is high. One investigation (Snow, 1958) found that only 14 per cent of blackbirds' nests in Wytham Woods resulted successfully in fledged young – a failure rate of 86 per cent, caused mainly by predators. Urban and suburban rates of success are better, but are highly variable according to location. The average survival rates appear to be between 20 and 50 per cent.

After leaving the nest the young birds are extremely vulnerable, particularly if there is insufficient cover to protect them against predators and inclement weather.

Human disturbance

Back at the nest site, human disturbance can easily cause desertion by the parents, especially up to and including the egg laying stage. Some species and individuals are more prone to desert than others: robins readily desert at an early stage. In nests of blackbirds and thrushes, disturbance can cause the chicks to erupt from the nest several days before they are due to fledge; leaving the nest too soon often means that they are unable to withstand cold nights. The message is to leave all nests alone. Do not disturb a nest, its contents or the adult birds.

When the young have left the nest, they should also be left alone. If the parents are not visible, it usually means they are either enjoying a well-deserved feed or they are collecting more food for their young. They will return and find their offspring when the coast is clear of predators and humans.

Nearly all birds are protected by law, especially during the breeding season, so it is illegal to disturb them at this time. Even those birdwatchers engaged in the Nest Records Scheme of the BTO have a strict set of rules governing their actions whilst they examine the progress of nests. These nest details are essential for the Scheme if it is to help in the monitoring and conservation of our wild birds.

Crack willow hybrid

Osier

(Above) *Salix* catkins are popular for nest foundations.

BIRDWATCHER'S TIP
‖‖‖

A birdwatcher's garden should provide a variety of nest materials. Some gardeners ensure this by scattering materials like scraps of wool, hair, feathers and other litter, or placing these in containers, to aid the nesters. Remember that some birds, including blackbirds and martins, also require water and mud.

Predators

The number of breeding birds lost to traffic is very large, and many more are lost to predators. A certain amount of predation is sustainable in most populations and is, in fact, desirable. With no natural checks, the population might increase beyond the sustainability of its resources, if it is not overcome by disease or by food shortages. If, however, the predators are not also kept under control, this imbalance would place the bird populations under threat.

Cats have a definite impact on wildlife. Based on a survey by the Mammal Society in 1997, it has been estimated that Britain's nine million cats caught between 25–29 million birds, 52–63 million mammals and 4–6 million reptiles and amphibians during the five months of the survey. Can this be sustainable?

Deterrents to keep cats away from nesting birds are difficult. One system is to spray any visiting cats from a can of water or the garden hose. Animals soon learn to avoid actions that involve getting wet. Owners of cats might try a cat bell, provided the cat will not get caught on a branch by its collar.

Unlike domestic cats, sparrowhawks and other birds of prey hunt to obtain food for themselves and their offspring; their numbers are regulated by food availability.

Weather conditions

Inclement weather, cold conditions, prolonged snow or rain, or conversely, a long, hot, dry spell, can and do cause nest desertion. If young birds become soaked in the nest, it can lead to chilling and death.

Adverse weather also affects the food supply because insects, and especially caterpillars, become scarce and provide insufficient food to keep young birds healthy. Blue tits will feed their young on peanut fragments when a shortage of natural foods leaves them desperate. This

Cats should be kept away from nesting birds. A cat bell can help to warn birds of an unwelcome visitor.

can lead to the death of nestling blue tits, as it can cause them to choke. Sadly, even without a peanut they would have starved to death.

Leaving sprinklers on to water lawns and borders may also water hedges and shrubs, causing any resident nestlings to become drenched, which can result in pneumonia.

CUTTING HEDGES

Hedges, in particular, can be a source of contention between neighbours when they become overgrown during the summer months. The best time for cutting a hedge is from September to before the end of March (in a late season). If the hedge is really inconvenient, a careful search must be carried out to ascertain that no nests will be disturbed. A gentle clip of the offending growth, performed quickly and quietly with a pair of secateurs, should reveal if there are any nests hidden. This clipping will usually suffice until the hedge can be cut back properly later. Cutting hedges mechanically is always more drastic and dangerous, especially if there are any early or late nests. Hand clipping can be stopped more quickly if an unsuspected nest is revealed.

TREES AS NEST SITES

Oak	Stock dove, woodpeckers, owls, redwing, blue + great tits, nuthatch, treecreeper, corvids, starling, tree sparrow, hawfinch
Ash	Great spotted + green woodpecker
Beech	Woodpeckers, redwing, great tit, nuthatch, corvids, starling
Cypress	Collared dove, blackbird, song thrush, goldcrest, bullfinch
Elm	Woodpeckers, nuthatch, corvids, finches (incl. redpoll)
Hornbeam	Woodpeckers, hawfinch, greenfinch, bullfinch
Larch	Magpie, goldcrest, siskin, goldfinch
Scots pine	Sparrowhawk, great spotted woodpecker, goldcrest, jay, siskin, redpoll
Spruce	Turtle + collared dove, goldcrest, coal tit, magpie, greenfinch, siskin, redpoll
Sycamore	Great spotted woodpecker, redwing, corvids, hawfinch

SMALLER TREES

Alder	Great + lesser spotted woodpecker, chaffinch, goldfinch, bullfinch, redpoll
Birch	Woodpeckers, redwing, goldcrest, crow, jay, hawfinch, redpoll
Cherry	Collared dove, blackbird, song thrush, black redstart, greenfinch
Conifers, indeterminate	Pigeon + doves, mistle thrush, lesser whitethroat, garden warbler, jay, chaffinch, crossbill, linnet, redpoll
Elder	Turtle dove, wren, mistle thrush, whitethroat, blackcap, garden warbler, goldcrest, linnet, redpoll, greenfinch, chaffinch
Holly	Dunnock, blackbird, long-tailed tit, jay, redpoll
Orchard trees	Turtle dove, green + lesser spotted woodpecker, mistle thrush, redstart, spotted flycatcher, goldfinch, hawfinch, chaffinch, redpoll
Willow (pollarded)	Lesser spotted woodpecker, pied wagtail, redwing, treecreeper, crow, redpoll
Yew	Goldcrest, magpie, goldfinch, greenfinch, bullfinch
Dead wood in trees, indeterminate	Many birds incl. owls, robin, redstart, flycatchers, tits, nuthatch, treecreeper, starling, sparrows

Abbreviations: Birds written in plural indicates several or most species within the family or group. Lack of space leads to grouping. For example, corvids includes carrion crow, rook, jackdaw, magpie and jay.

HEDGES, BUSHES AND SMALL TREES AS NEST SITES

Hawthorn	Turtle dove, blackbird, song thrush, blackcap, garden warbler, whitethroats, long-tailed tit, jay, finches (incl. linnet, redpoll)
Blackthorn	Turtle dove, blackcap, garden warbler, whitethroats, long-tailed tit, hawfinch, bullfinch, chaffinch
Bamboo	Greenfinch
Berberis	Long-tailed tit
Bird cherry	Greenfinch, chaffinch
Box	Dunnock, goldcrest, greenfinch, bullfinch
Cotoneaster	Blackbird, other thrushes
Forsythia	Song thrush, linnet
Gorse	Dunnock, redwing, blackcap, garden warbler, whitethroats, long-tailed tit, linnet, redpoll
Hedging cypress	Blackbird, other thrushes, dunnock, finches
Loganberries	Wren, blackbird, blackcap
Lonicera nitida	Dunnock, blackbird, song thrush
Privet	Blackbird, song thrush
Pyracantha	Song thrush
Rhododendron + laurel	Redwing, bullfinch
Rose	Warblers
Sea buckthorn	Redpoll
Snowberry/ivy	Dunnock, blackbird, song thrush, jay, blackcap, bullfinch
Hedge stock	Blackbird, song thrush, whitethroats, linnet, redpoll
Ornamental shrubs	Blackbird, song thrush, chaffinch, greenfinch

CLIMBING PLANTS AS NEST SITES

Clematis	Blackbird, blackcap, long-tailed tit, goldfinch, greenfinch, linnet
Honeysuckle	Goldcrest, blackcap, long-tailed tit
Ivy on walls	Spotted flycatcher, willow warbler, chiffchaff, long-tailed tit, goldfinch
Rose	Goldfinch
Virginia creeper	Spotted flycatcher, goldfinch
Wisteria	Spotted flycatcher, thrushes
Other creepers + climbers	Thrushes, bullfinch, chaffinch

HERBACEOUS PLANTS, GROUND COVER AND BASE OF HEDGEROWS AS NEST SITES

Brambles	Tree pipit, dunnock, blackbird, blackcap, garden warbler, whitethroats, chiffchaff, long-tailed tit, chaffinch, bullfinch, linnet
Bracken	Pheasant, tree pipit, blackbird, garden warbler, willow warbler
Briars	Dunnock, garden warbler, whitethroat, chaffinch
Ferns	Garden warbler, chaffinch
Grassy banks	Tree pipit, garden + willow warbler, whitethroat
Heather	Twite, linnet
Hedge bottoms	Pheasant, partridge, blackcap, willow warbler
Ivy over tree stumps, etc.	Wren, robin, chaffinch
Nettles	Blackcap, garden warbler, whitethroat
Strawberries	Tree pipit

PLANT MATERIALS USED IN THE FOUNDATIONS AND BODY OF NESTS

MATERIALS	TYPE	BIRDS
Wood + twigs		
	Birch	Sparrowhawk, crow, redwing, treecreeper
	Larch	Sparrowhawk
	Beech	Rook
	Apple	Crow
	Oak	Crow, hawfinch
Twigs, sticks	Indeterminate	Pigeons, doves, corvids, finches incl. crossbill
Fine twigs		Pigeons, pied wagtail, song thrush, treecreeper, finches
Bark		Jackdaw, flycatchers, nuthatch, treecreeper, crossbill, chaffinch
Plant stems		
Stiff stalks	Galium	Woodpigeon, collared dove, yellowhammer
		Blackcap, garden warbler
	Ivy	Treecreeper
Fibres		Redstarts, chiffchaff, spotted flycatcher, chaffinch
Leaves		
	Beech	Nuthatch
	Oak	Dunnock, pied flycatcher, nuthatch
	Dead	Wren, robin, warblers, redpoll
Grass		Swift, hirundines, pied wagtail, dunnock, thrushes incl. robin, warblers, tits, starling, sparrow, finches, buntings
Straw		Stock dove, swallow, starling, sparrows
Fronds	Bracken + fern	Wren, willow warbler, pied flycatcher
Rootlets		
		Doves, pied wagtail, dunnock, redstart, treecreeper, finches, buntings
Seed + catkins		
	Oak	Spotted flycatcher
	Willow	Redpoll
	Plant down, hairy seeds	Crossbill
	Honesty seed heads	Blackbird
Moss + lichens		
	Hypnum (moss)	Long-tailed tit
	Usnea barbata (lichen)	Magpie
	Indeterminate	Wren, dunnock, thrushes (incl. robin), warblers, spotted flycatcher, tits, treecreeper, finches, buntings

NON-PLANT MATERIALS USED IN THE FOUNDATIONS AND BODY OF NESTS

MATERIALS	TYPE	BIRDS
Natural		
	Saliva	Swift, song thrush
	Spider cocoons	Redpoll
	Cobwebs	Long-tailed tit, blackcap, goldcrest, goldfinch
	Peat	House martin, song thrush
	Mud + earth	Corvids, hirundines, thrushes, nuthatch
	Hair	Long-tailed tit, marsh tit, howfinch, bullfinch, crossbill, yellowhammer
	Fur + wool	Mistle thrush, redwing, blackcap, flycatchers, finches
Man-made		
	String	Jackdaw, mistle thrush, blue tit, crossbill
	Binder twine, raffia	Jackdaw, collared dove, blackbird, house sparrow
	Paper	Mistle thrush, crossbill, chaffinch
	Debris, plastics, rubbish	Owls, corvids

NEST LINING MATERIALS

MATERIALS	TYPE	BIRDS
Leaves		Sparrowhawk, rook, wren
	Dead	Woodcock
Grass	Fine, incl. bent	Collared dove, hirundines, tree pipit, mistle thrush, redwing, warblers
Rootlets	Fine	Robin, blackcap, garden warbler, flycatchers, corvids, greenfinch, siskin
Seeds + catkins	Down	House martin, marsh tit, siskin, linnet, redpoll
Moss		Rook, wren, dunnock, pied flycatcher
	Moss flowers	Robin
Cobweb		Serin, house sparrow
Hair		Pied wagtail, dunnock, redstarts, warblers, flycatchers, tits, treecreeper, corvids, finches
Fur		Jackdaw, coal tit, marsh tit
Wool		Pied wagtail, dunnock, flycatchers, blue tit, treecreeper, corvids, sparrow, twite
Feathers		Sparrowhawk, swift, hirundines, pied wagtail, wren, dunnock, redstarts, warblers, goldcrest, flycatchers, tits + long-tailed tit, treecreeper, starling, sparrow, finches

NEST RIM ORNAMENTS

MATERIALS	TYPE	BIRDS
Wood chips	Birch bark	Chaffinch
Ivy		Mistle thrush
Flower petals + seeds		Mistle thrush
Seed down		Whitethroat
Lichens		Spotted flycatcher
Cobwebs		Blackcap, lesser whitethroat, spotted flycatcher, chaffinch
Wool		Mistle thrush, blackcap, lesser whitethroat, greenfinch
Feathers		Mistle thrush, greenfinch
Rags + paper		Mistle thrush, spotted flycatcher
String		Spotted flycatcher
Confetti + other man-made scraps		Chaffinch

FEEDING HABITS

The majority of birds need both plant and animal food. Each species has its own requirements and the winter diet is usually very different from the summer diet. Autumn, the time of plenty, is when most species stock up on food, laying it down as fat, against either a strenuous migration or the restricted food supplies of winter.

Plants

The plants in a garden are a potential food source for birds. Quite a few trees are liked for their sap. Some plants have edible fruits, berries or seeds that provide seasonal food, and others have buds, shoots, leaves, and even roots and tubers. These are mainly vegetables. It tends to be the larger birds that attack roots and tubers, and many are adept at demolishing crops. Woodpigeons are the greatest culprits here, but geese are also troublesome in some areas. Bullfinches and sparrows enjoy tree buds and flowers in spring, whilst blackbirds and house sparrows partake of yellow crocuses. Nectar and pollen add valuable protein to a bird's diet, especially in spring when other food is short.

A woodpigeon feeds on seed, grain and berries and can devastate crops if given access.

Ash (*Fraxinus excelsior*) keys

(Left) Seeds of the ash are food for finches and wood pigeons. Bullfinches, which can be pests in orchards, seem to ignore the fruit tree flower buds in years when there is a bumper crop of ash keys.

Guelder rose (*Viburnum opulus*)

(Below) Many maple seeds are taken by finches and pigeons, whilw oozing tree sap is relished by small tits.

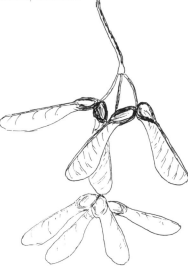

Sycomore (*Acer pseudoplatanus*) keys

In our garden, blue and great tits regularly visit the flowering currant bushes to extract nectar, whilst house sparrows and blue tits seek pollen and nectar from the cotoneaster flowers in June. Waxwings and woodpeckers are known to take sap from young tree shoots.

Many birds – blackcaps, greenfinches and chaffinches – consume a huge range of plant foods, so there is scope for a great deal more observation on the exact plants that birds will eat, either rarely (in times of general food shortage) or regularly, when available.

Plants are also an essential indirect supplier of food. They attract insects, spiders and many other invertebrates that depend on them either for food or for reproductive purposes. Plants, in turn, benefit from insects. Many plants depend on insects for their reproduction, with visiting insects being responsible for pollination. Even vertebrates, including lizards, frogs and mammals, use plants for food and shelter. These animals in turn provide food for the larger birds of prey, notably owls, hawks and falcons.

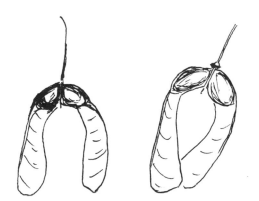

Cultivated forms with greater and lesser angled positions

(Below) Seed heads of Aquilegia species

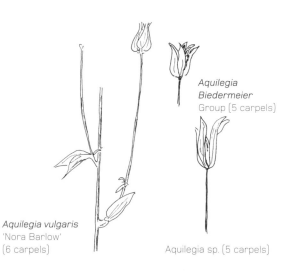

Aquilegia Biedermeier Group (5 carpels)

Aquilegia vulgaris 'Nora Barlow' (6 carpels)

Aquilegia sp. (5 carpels)

Norway maple (*Acer platanoides*) and field maple (*Acer campestre*) with horizontal wings

A blackbird has been busily consuming these *Photinia* berries.

Availability

Cultivated fruits and berries can be made available for 11 months of the year by carefully selecting the varieties grown. During May, when fruit is scarcest and there is a dramatic rise in insect abundance, most birds eat less plant material and more insects. Weed seeds also are indispensable at this time.

When there is a choice, some individual birds will decimate their favourite food before touching anything else but others will try to keep their favourite in reserve and defend it against all other potential competitors.

Seed dispersal

Fruit consumption by birds and mammals is an effective method of spreading plant species. Many birds are attracted to bright, fleshy fruits. If these are swallowed whole, the seeds will remain intact, and will later be passed through and expelled from the bird's body. If they land in suitable conditions, the seeds will germinate and grow into new plants, some distance from the parent. Birds that disseminate seeds in this way are known as fruit dispersers. However, not all fruit-eating birds assist plants in this way. Some eat the fleshy pulp, leaving the seed attached to its parent, whilst others chew up the seeds, rendering them useless.

GREENFINCH

Greenfinches often chew seeds away from the fleshy parts of fruit, and therefore do not assist plant distribution in the same way as some other fruit-eating birds. However, seed predators such as greenfinches occasionally do eat a whole seed, and if it passes through the bird unharmed, there is the possibility of a new plant. We have three Daphne mezereum plants that have turned up in odd corners, probably courtesy of the greenfinch. A third, unhelpful practice is to eat all the fruits before they ripen! Greenfinches appear to eat mostly unripe daphne berries, leaving no chance for reproduction.

Insects

Breeding is timed to coincide with the greatest abundance of food; this occurs when the insect population is at its peak. Many seed eaters turn to a high protein insect diet during the spring and summer when they are rearing their offspring. However, to survive throughout the year on insects, they would have to migrate to warmer climes for the winter or they would probably perish for lack of food.

Many very young birds are fed on aphids, but as they develop they are given a more varied diet that may include other insects, earthworms, molluscs, crustaceans and some plant material.

BIRDWATCHER'S TIP

During difficult winter conditions, a lot of birds survive only by eating food quite alien to their normal diet. More observation is needed to ascertain food preferences and which foods are eaten only in times of scarcity.

KEY

Fish	
Aquatic plants	
Mammals	
Insects	
Eggs	
Crustaceans	
Carrion	
Amphibians and Reptiles	
Birds	
Invertebrates	
Seeds/cereals	
Vegetables	
Fruit	
Nuts	
Nectar/pollen	

Herons tend to stalk their food by standing motionless at the water's edge. It eats mainly fish.

Directory of general bird feeding habits

Grebes and herons

Gardens with a river may have a little grebe looking for small fish, crustacea and molluscs. Grey heron, especially young birds, will visit ornamental ponds in gardens. They mainly eat fish, including goldfish, but also frogs, reptiles, voles and occasionally young birds or worms. Very little plant material is taken.

Wildfowl, geese, ducks and swans

All are plant grazers. The mallard is the most frequent garden visitor but the omnivorous tufted duck will visit ornamental ponds, even in cities. The mallard eats cereals and other seeds, even acorns, but the tufted duck can dive for fish and will also consume molluscs and shrimps, but eats mostly aquatic plants.

Greylag and Canada geese may visit gardens adjoining rivers, where they will happily gorge on a large variety of plants including cereals, grasses and brassicas. They will also eat the roots and tubers of other vegetables. Mute swans and other ducks may also appear occasionally at waterside gardens.

Sparrowhawks and kestrels

These are the two most likely birds of prey to be seen in gardens, although red kites are known to take carrion put out for them in a few gardens. The female sparrowhawk, being larger than the male, is more likely to penetrate further into towns, as she is able to take larger prey. She can swoop around a corner, making an unexpected catch at a bird table but fortunately not always succeeding! Sparrowhawks eat mammals, including voles, rats, young rabbits and even squirrels.

Mallards inhabit ponds and rivers, grazing on the leaves and shoots of water plants as well as taking acorns, cereals, seeds and invertebrates.

Greylag geese are occasional visitors to gardens near an area of water, and feed on grass, roots and cereals.

The moorhen can often be found in town parks. It feeds on plants, seeds, fruit, berries, grasses and occasionally snails.

Kestrels take fewer birds; they feed mainly on small mammals including rabbits, but also on earthworms, insects in flight, earwigs and frogs. In winter they have been known to eat apples.

Partridges and pheasants

Grey partridges feed mainly in open fields but may shelter by the garden hedge, whilst the red-legged partridge is more attracted to orchards. Both consume grasses, cereals and weed seeds, and also aphids, beetles, ants and bugs.

The pheasant is a more frequent garden visitor with a more varied diet, eating nuts and fruits including hazelnut, hawthorn, blackthorn, apple and raspberry. They will dig up bulbs and roots and also consume woodlice, millipedes, earthworms, slugs, snails and voles.

Rails, crakes and coots

The omnivorous water rail is common throughout wetland habitats in the UK but very shy and rare in gardens. Corncrake are only found in the Outer Hebridies. They consume many insects, including dragonflies, flies and beetles, and will also eat earwigs, spiders and earthworms. The rail will eat eggs, small birds, mammals and sometimes breadcrumbs, and both eat some plant material.

Coots eat more snails and small mammals than moorhens; both will eat spiders, flies, bugs, caddisflies and moths. They will also eat the leaves of many water plants, including duckweed, *Potamogeton*, reedmace and water lilies. The moorhen will eat tree and shrub berries, rowan, yew, ivy, hawthorn, apples and pears, whereas the coot specializes in aquatic algae.

Gulls

Gulls are well-known for piracy and scavenging, but will also consume berries and other plant material, together with mice, voles, small birds and eggs. Black-headed, herring, common and great black-backed gulls used to turn up regularly for scraps from an inland rooftop balcony. We also saw a lesser black-backed gull there on one occasion. A large part of the black-headed gull's diet consists of earthworms and insects.

The black-headed gull is a coastal bird, often found inland where there is plenty of food. It eats fish, worms and insects.

Pigeons and doves

All eat mostly plant material but they will also occasionally eat worms, small snails, spiders and insects. Feral, woodpigeon and stock dove will eat slugs and all the family, including collared and turtle dove, eat cereal and weed seeds and fruit. The turtle dove will not readily eat from a bird table.

Ring-necked parakeet

These birds are successful in southern suburban gardens. They are fond of apples, peanuts, berried shrubs, young peas and bird seed.

Woodpigeons can be seen in parks and gardens where they eat mainly seeds, green leaves and berries.

Cuckoos

Cuckoos are mainly insectivorous but will also eat some slugs, snails and spiders, and the berries of bilberry, buckthorn and juniper.

Owls

Barn, tawny and little owls eat a wide variety of mammals, some birds, frogs, toads, lizards, and a few fish, insects, snails and earthworms. The tawny owl is recorded as having the greatest variety of prey, whilst the little owl will occasionally eat berries, maize and grass leaves.

Swifts

Swifts feed on the wing. They will devour flying insects including flies, ants and bees.

The ring-necked parakeet eats fruit, nuts, seeds and berries. Some will also eat bacon rind from bird tables.

Kingfishers

Kingfishers occasionally visit garden ponds and will devour fish, eels, frogs and insects, including dragonflies. They will also consume a little aquatic vegetation.

Bee-eaters and hoopoe

Climate change could bring more of these birds northwards across from the continent: Bee-eaters successfully bred in County Durham in 2002. Both species like orchards, feeding on bees and wasps and many other invertebrates and plant food. Hoopoe will eat elderberries and small seeds.

Woodpeckers

The smallest and least observed woodpecker, the lesser spotted, always feeds on insects above ground level, mostly beetles, moths, aphids, ants and wasps. It will occasionally visit orchards to eat raspberries, currants and peas. The larger green woodpecker will demolish ant colonies and will also eat bugs, beetles, earwigs, flies, earthworms, snails and tree seeds as well as fruit, including apples, cherries and *Pyracantha* berries. Apart from insects, woodlice, earthworms and bird table food, woodpeckers will also eat gooseberries, currants, cherries and juniper seeds.

Our own garden is frequently visited by great spotted woodpeckers. Green woodpeckers are comparatively scarce in the region. The great spotted woodpecker takes insects when available but also eats tree seeds in winter and the eggs and nestlings of other birds in spring and summer. Woodpeckers will drill holes in nest boxes to extract the young. We watched a male bird tapping a nest box that had young great tits inside. He waited until a youngster's head went up towards the hole, then dived in with his beak and extracted the nestling. He then took the small

A kingfisher may visit a garden pond if it is large enough, but kingfishers are normally found near lakes and rivers, where they dive for fish and aquatic insects.

The skylark feeds mainly on insects, seeds and grains. It is found mostly in the countryside, but occasionally visits gardens.

The swallow is found in places where there is a good supply of insects. They especially enjoy flies.

The pied wagtail feeds on small invertebrates it finds on the ground or by 'flycatching' in the air.

bird to a larger hole a few yards away and ate it. We have also found young starling remains in this hole. The females we have seen have not been quite so destructive, but the sexes do not appear to tolerate each other near a feeding place.

 Skylark

Skylarks are dependent on insects during the summer, together with a few spiders, slugs and snails. They also eat leaves and seeds, including grasses, dock, buttercup, poppy, vetches and daisies. In winter they sometimes visit gardens to supplement their diet. Skylarks have greatly reduced in numbers in our countryside. If insects are removed from the farmland, where will skylarks go?

Hirundines, swallows, sand and house martins

All of these summer visitors feed on insects. If pollution levels increase in a town, house martins will depart. Swallows also prefer a more rural aspect, with plenty of flying insects. Sand martins can only be expected to visit a garden if it adjoins a river with sandy banks and, again, plenty of insects. All hirundines like to eat mayflies, damsel flies, flies, moths, bugs, beetles, ants and spiders.

 Pipits and wagtails

Mostly insectivorous feeders, these will consume anything from dragonflies to ants and aphids. The meadow pipit will eat an occasional earthworm, and both grey and pied wagtails will partake of minnows. In winter all may visit bird tables. The pied wagtail will eat a few weed seeds but the meadow pipit eats a much wider variety of plant food, including violets, figwort, crowberry, grasses, rushes and sedges.

Waxwings

The waxwing is an irruptive winter visitor, when it feeds mainly on fruits, berries, buds and flowers. It will eat insects when available, flying up suddenly from a branch to catch one aerially. The variety of plant food they can eat is quite large. Very often a flock will descend onto a group of berried bushes, busily and noisily demolishing practically all the berries; we watched one group with over 60 birds. Sometimes a single bird will drop down to eat the few remaining cotoneaster berries left on a hedge. The waxwing is also extremely fond of rowan and whitebeam berries; unfortunately, most of our rowan berries have been eaten long before the waxwings arrive!

The wren is a regular garden visitor. Wrens eat insects and spiders but will also take small seeds.

 Wrens

Mainly insectivorous, wrens will eat anything from mayflies, grasshoppers, earwigs, aphids, sawflies and beetles to spiders, mites, woodlice and even tadpoles! Their plant foods include raspberries and seeds.

 Dunnocks

Dunnocks will eat more seeds and berries than wrens, but are still mainly insectivorous, consuming grasshoppers, butterflies, earwigs, bugs, moths, ants and beetles. They will also eat spiders, a few snails, earthworms, and seeds and berries including nettle, dock, buttercup, pinks, bramble, elder and holly.

The dunnock is often found close to the ground in woodland, parks and gardens looking for spiders, worms and insects.

 Thrushes

This family has many members that visit or live in gardens. It can be subdivided into two groups: the first comprising the robin, the nightingale, redstarts, chats and possibly the ring ouzel; the second comprising the blackbird and four spotted thrushes, song and mistle thrush, redwing and the fieldfare. Insects constitute

The song thrush is found in woods, hedgerows, parks and gardens. It feeds on worms, fruit, snails and insects.

a large part of the summer diet of the first group, especially tipulids or crane flies, *Lepidoptera* (moths and butterflies) larvae, and beetles. The robin, redstarts and the ring ouzel are especially fond of spiders, earwigs, thrips, ants, woodlice, slugs and earthworms. In autumn, fruits are also eaten. The nightingale and ring ouzel might be observed eating elderberries, but the whinchat remains mainly an insect eater.

(Below) The fieldfare is found in the countryside, especially in fields and hedges. It feeds on insects, worms and berries.

(Above) The redwing is found in fields and hedges but will visit parks and gardens where it looks for worms and berries.

Blackbirds, song and mistle thrushes can be seen throughout the year even though the latter two may partially migrate during hard winters. All eat many insects and invertebrates, including spiders, woodlice, snails, slugs and earthworms. It has been estimated that a song thrush will eat over 10,000 caterpillars, flies, snails and grubs in the breeding season. The blackbird and mistle thrush occasionally eat small fish and nestlings but in late summer they eat more fruit and berries. The song thrush eats smaller berries than the other two, which are both bigger and more aggressive to other birds.

The winter visitors, redwing and fieldfare, eat invertebrates when available and also fruit and berries. They come into gardens mainly when the weather deteriorates. Those gardens nearer wooded areas appear to attract redwings more than fieldfares, which seem to prefer a more open habitat. If conditions are hard, both species come to our garden, otherwise we see mainly redwings. The redwing cannot swallow the larger berries liked by the blackbird and fieldfare and this restricts its diet slightly. All thrushes appreciate apples on the ground, especially in bad weather.

Warblers

Warblers, including the goldcrest and firecrest, live mainly on insects. Some, such as the sedge warbler that can breed in neglected orchards, live on insects but sample a little fruit – elderberries and blackberries – in the autumn. Others consume a greater variety of seasonal fruits, including cherry, raspberry and currant. One August we watched an icterine warbler in the garden hunting for insects, then unexpectedly plucking and devouring a whole rowan berry.

Rose hips are enjoyed by hungry thrushes.

Whitethroat and lesser whitethroat also eat more berries and fruit from late summer. Records show that they will eat bilberry, hawthorn, daphne, buckthorn, plum and viburnum. The whitethroat also eats the seeds of bryony, bindweed, honeysuckle and asparagus, among others. The garden warbler is similar but consumes more seeds and fruits, including spindle, Clematis, dogwood, ivy and birch. It will also take nectar from *Fritillaria* and maple and pollen from hawthorn. The blackcap, other than during the breeding season, has the greatest variety in diet, eating many more fruits, including strawberry, chokeberry, quince, snowberry, cotoneaster and *Pyracantha*, and the seeds of weeds, herbaceous plants, shrubs and trees. It will also take nectar from trees, including willow, and is a regular bird-table visitor.

The smaller warblers, wood, willow and chiffchaff, are mainly insectivorous but will sample a little autumn fruit – notably elder, currant, bilberry, blackberry, raspberry and alder buckthorn.

 The vagrant yellow-browed warbler, as well as hunting for insects under sycamore leaves in gardens on the east coast, will eat spiders, small molluscs and a few seeds. The goldcrest and firecrest are similar, but both will eat breadcrumbs, and the goldcrest will also eat pine and spruce seeds.

Flycatchers

Pied and spotted flycatchers catch insects aerially, especially ants and flies. They also take dragonflies, grasshoppers, earwigs, bugs, moths, beetles, spiders, woodlice, snails and earthworms. The spotted flycatcher will eat the fruit of currant, cherry, viburnum, dogwood and blackberry, and both will eat daphne, *Amelanchier*, buckthorn and elder.

The long-tailed tit is constantly on the move as it searches for insects, which are supplemented by seeds in the autumn and winter.

Long-tailed tits

These tits eat a variety of insects, including grasshoppers, aphids, flies, moths, beetles and ants, as well as spiders and snails. In the autumn and winter they will supplement this diet with the seeds of privet, birch, alder and sunflowers, and food from bird tables.

Tits from the family Paridae

Blue, coal, crested, marsh, willow and great tits are mainly insectivorous during the breeding season. Each pair of birds removes thousands of caterpillars to feed even one brood. Estimates vary, but one puts the number of caterpillars taken by a pair of great tits to feed each brood at 7,000 to 8,000. The frequency with which blue and great tits will take food into a nest box containing young is very high.

Marsh and willow tits consume earwigs, aphids, mayflies, wasps, ants, beetles, spiders, snails and earthworms. Both eat the seeds from conifers and deciduous trees, the willow tit usually eating the smaller seeds. The marsh tit also eats crab apple, hawthorn and chestnut, and the willow tit will eat berries. Both like pollen and sap from trees such as alder and maple and will rarely visit bird tables.

The crested tit, although it has a confined distribution, does occur in some Scottish gardens outside the breeding season. It eats mostly conifer seeds but also likes rowan and the sap of birch.

The coal tit is similar, eating insects and spiders in summer, with a seed supplement, especially spruce, in autumn and winter. It also likes sap, pollen and even moss capsules!

Not a common garden bird, the willow tit is usually found in alder, birch and willow woodland near water where it feeds on insects, seeds and berries.

The blue tit is commonly seen in gardens looking for insects, seeds and nuts. It is also a frequent visitor to bird feeders.

Food lists for blue and great tits are longer, probably because they are more adaptable and because they have been the subject of more intensive study. They consume a large number of insects and spiders during the summer, but from autumn onwards eat many more seeds and fruits. Blue tits also like pollen and the nectar of various trees and shrubs.

Nuthatches

Nuthatches devour large numbers of insects and other invertebrates. When not breeding they eat more seeds and fruits, the buds of trees such as pine, spruce, yew, hazel, beech and oak, the fruits of cherry, pear, blackberry and *Berberis*, nuts, and bird table food.

Treecreepers

Treecreepers have a finer bill than nuthatches, so they eat mostly insects and spiders along with a few seeds from pine, spruce and juniper, apple and bilberry. They will also take fat from bird feeding stations.

Golden orioles

Golden orioles are very scare but may visit large gardens where, during spring and summer, they will consume large insects, spiders and molluscs. In autumn and winter they will eat carrion, fruit, berries and the buds of conifers, blackberries, fruit trees, rowan and elder.

Red-backed shrike

This shrike used to inhabit overgrown gardens but now it is only a rare migrant. As a 'butcher bird' it eats meat, spearing its prey (moths, beetles, mice and small reptiles) onto thorn bushes (its larder). It also eats the fruit of elder, cherry and rose.

Gardens near woodlands, parks or overgrown cemeteries may have nuthatches as frequent visitors to bird tables.

Another woodland bird, the treecreeper, eats mainly insects and spiders and is only occasionally seen at feeding stations.

Corvids or crows

Members of this family – the jay, magpie, jackdaw, rook and carrion crow – have all visited our garden. Some come daily, others less frequently. All are opportunists and scavengers. All consume insects, especially beetles and moth and butterfly larvae. The rook spends more time hunting for earthworms but will also eat other invertebrates and even small mammals and birds.

We were slightly surprised when a jackdaw attacked a collared dove that was sitting tight on her nest, and nearly killed her before dropping her from mid-air. Sadly, our neighbours were not successful in their attempts to rescue her. On another occasion a pair of jackdaws attacked a young dove and, although disturbed, they returned later. All corvids seem to show this persistence!

The plant diet of this family includes the seeds and fruits of trees and shrubs, including blackberry, hawthorn and elder, nuts, which are especially liked by jays, weed seeds and cereals.

Starlings

Starlings are omnivorous. They will eat frogs and insects, in particular leather-jackets, carrion and nestlings, as well as spiders, woodlice and earthworms. They will also eat both cultivated and wild plant seeds and fruits and even dandelion flowers! The rare, rose-coloured starling apparently eats smaller insects, along with fruit and grasses.

Sparrows

Young sparrows are fed mainly on insects, whilst adults eat mostly plant food. Tree sparrows may eat more fruit than the house sparrow but all consume a wide variety of plant material, including buds, berries, and the seeds of a range of plants from trees to cereals. Tree sparrows are shy and rare, but both they and house sparrows can be seen in gardens.

The rook is a scavenger, often found in fields or by the roadside. It eats insects, worms and cereals.

Jackdaws are present in gardens throughout the year and can dominate feeding stations.

A starling is a common garden bird and will eat almost anything, including insects, worms, fruits and seeds.

Finches

Finches can be subdivided according to their feeding habits, which are related to bill shape and size. Chaffinch and brambling are very similar, consuming insects, from dragonflies to beetles, during the breeding season. Brambling will also eat seeds, gathered by opening cones, at this time. They both eat seeds, mostly gathered from the ground. The brambling's bill is slightly larger than that of the chaffinch and it eats more beech mast, but both finches like tree seeds, some fruits and grass seeds. They will also occasionally eat millipedes, worms and snails.

The serin, and also the canary, which is often found as an escapee, feed mainly on seeds from trees and weeds, but the young are fed on aphids, caterpillars and spiders.

Both the siskin and the goldfinch have long, narrow beaks, which they use to extract seeds by probing them into tree cones and Compositae seed heads; the larger-beaked goldfinch can probe deeper into teasel heads. The goldfinch also eats more grass seeds and weeds from open country than the siskin. Both partake of insects during the breeding season.

The redpoll, linnet, twite and greenfinch have broader bills. The redpoll has the smallest of the three and the greenfinch the largest. The redpoll therefore eats the smallest seeds, like birch, whilst the greenfinch eats larger tree seeds and cereals. The linnet specializes in farmland weeds and the similar-sized twite eats weeds and a few tree seeds. As to insects, flies and beetles, the twite consumes a limited variety whilst breeding, compared with the linnet, the greenfinch still more and the redpoll the most.

You are unlikely to see a chaffinch on a bird feeder, but you may spot it under a bird table looking for food.

The siskin has a narrow beak that it uses to extract seeds from conifer, birch and alder trees.

The goldfinch's beak allows it to extract seeds from thistles and teasels in the same way as the siskin.

Crossbills, including the Scottish crossbill, eat the fewest invertebrates. The Scottish crossbill likes conifer seeds, mostly pine. The common crossbill prefers spruce but will eat the seeds of deciduous trees, grasses and dandelions, and also apple, rowan, ivy and honeysuckle.

The common rosefinch eats spiders, insects and seeds, fruits from trees and shrubs, cultivated plants and weeds. It will also eat sedges and grasses.

The bullfinch, with its short, stubby beak, feeds its young mainly on insects (aphids, moths, flies and beetles) and spiders. It eats plants by systematically stripping fruit tree buds and devouring fleshy fruits, rowan, blackberry, guelder rose and seeds, including poppy, chickweed and dandelion. In our garden, bullfinches used to strip flower buds each year from the first apple varieties, then prunus, followed by clematis, jasmine, honeysuckle and then later varieties of apple.

The hawfinch has a large beak with which to tackle many hard tree seeds, including conifers, hazel, walnut and oak. It also enjoys the shoots of large trees and shrubs, peas, beans and dandelions. The young eat moth caterpillars and other insects.

The redpoll feeds among the branches of trees on small seeds, and occasionally it also eats insects.

The linnet is a heathland bird, but is occasionally seen in parks and gardens. It normally feeds on seeds on the ground.

(Below) The greenfinch is becoming a frequent garden visitor, where it takes full advantage if peanuts are on offer.

(Below left) The bullfinch eats seeds, buds and fruits and will eat from a hanging seed feeder. It also feeds on insects.

Buntings

The yellowhammer, cirl, reed and corn buntings consume many insects during their breeding cycle. The insects they will eat include grasshoppers, aphids, moths, flies, ants and beetles. Other invertebrates eaten include snails, spiders and earthworms. The yellowhammer prefers starchy seed, weeds, grasses and a few tree seeds. The cirl bunting feeds on weeds, grass and cereal seeds at or near ground level, whilst the reed bunting has a more varied diet that includes tree and other plant seeds, grasses and rushes. All will visit gardens for food in harsh conditions. The corn bunting will forage in rough grass but may use garden hedges in rural settings as singing posts. With its large beak, it can eat the seeds and buds of ivy, sycamore, Virginia creeper and broom as well as grass and cereals.

The reed bunting normally lives on marshland but can be found in gardens in winter. They eat seeds and insects.

Plants to attract feeding birds

The sheer number of plants eaten by birds prohibits us from including them all. The plants listed in the tables on pages 72–77 are examples of species that attract the widest variety of birds Other plants, not listed, may be consumed more often, but are a food source for a limited number of specific species.

For the same reason, we have given generic names only for most plants, and generally refer just to the genera and not the species. Many genera have numerous species, for example, *Ranunculus*, which has various well-known buttercup species (including bulbous buttercup, *R. bulbosus*, creeping buttercup, *R. repens* and field buttercup, *R. acris*), but the genus also includes lesser celandine, *R. ficaria*, lesser spearwort, *R. flammula* and water crowfoot, *R. aquatilis*. It is probable, though not certain, that if the seeds of any of these members of the genus are available then the birds listed, including ducks, geese, skylarks, finches and buntings, will consume them if they need food supplies. Generally, birds have been grouped under families, but wherever possible, more specific identifications have been given. For example, if a large number of warbler species eat a certain food, then the number of species is provided immediately after the group: warblers 12. When several species eat the food, the family name is given in the plural. If only one species eats the food, either the family name is in the singular or the individual is named.

We have included some avian rarities because bird populations aren't constant. Apart from climatic changes, there are many other factors that influence the spread and interaction of species, including the availability of wildlife corridors, competition for territories, food and shelter, and the presence of predators. The rarities of today may become abundant in a few years. As an example, the collared dove, quite rare at the end of the 1950s, is now a widespread breeder.

A coal tit will forage for insects and spiders amongst the foliage of trees and shrubs

SMALL TREES, SHRUBS AND CLIMBERS

PROVIDING FOOD FOR THE GREATEST VARIETY OF BIRDS

Alder, *Alnus*	Mallard, waxwing, fieldfare, tits (incl. long-tailed), tree sparrow, finches 13, reed bunting
Alder buckthorn, *Frangula*	Cuckoo, waxwing, thrushes 3 + redstarts 2, warblers, flycatchers, golden oriole, magpie, finches
Barberry, *Berberis*	Waxwing, thrushes 4, warblers, flycatcher, tits, nuthatch, corvids, greenfinch + hawfinch
Birch, *Betula*	Water rail, great spotted woodpecker, waxwing, dunnock, fieldfare, warblers, tits, corvids, sparrow, finches 13, bunting
Blackthorn, *Prunus spinosa*	Pheasant, pigeon, waxwing, thrushes (inc. robin), corvids, starling, finches
Buckthorn, *Rhamnus*	Moorhen, pigeon, cuckoo, great spotted woodpecker, waxwing, thrushes (incl. robin + redstart), warblers, flycatchers, tits, golden oriole, corvids, starling, finches
Cotoneaster spp.	Ring-necked parakeet, thrushes (incl. robin), blackcap, corvids, starling, sparrow, finches
Daphne spp.	Pheasant, blackbird, black redstart, warblers (incl. whitethroat), pied flycatcher, corvids, finches
Dogwood, *Cornus*	Woodpigeon, green woodpecker, waxwing, thrushes (incl. redstarts), warblers, spotted flycatcher, tits, golden oriole, corvids, starling, finches
Elder, *Sambucus*	Moorhen, black-headed gull, pigeon/dove, hoopoe, waxwing, wren, dunnock, thrushes (incl. robin), redstarts, warblers 12, flycatchers, tits, golden oriole, red-backed shrike, corvids, starling, sparrow, finches 12
Firethorn, *Pyracantha*	Green woodpecker, waxwing, thrushes, blackcap, starling, sparrow, greenfinch
Guelder rose, *Viburnum opulus*	Dove, waxwing, thrushes (incl. robin), blackcap, garden warbler, marsh tit, jay, finches
Hawthorn, *Crataegus*	Pheasant, moorhen, black-headed gull, waxwing, thrushes (incl. robin + black redstart), warblers, tits, golden oriole, corvids, starling, finches
Hazel, *Corylus*	Pheasant, woodpigeon, great spotted woodpecker, tits, nuthatch, jay, jackdaw, crossbill, hawfinch
Holly, *Ilex*	Woodpigeon, waxwing, dunnock, thrushes (incl. robin), blackcap, corvids, bullfinch, hawfinch
Honeysuckle, *Lonicera*	Waxwing, robin, blackbird, song thrush, black redstart, warblers, flycatcher, tits, corvids, starling, finches
Ivy, *Hedera*	Moorhen, pigeon/dove, waxwing, thrushes (incl. ring ouzel), warblers, golden oriole, corvids, starling, finches, corn bunting
June berry, *Amelanchier*	Waxwing, redstart, warblers, pied flycatcher, coal tit, golden oriole, corvid, starling, finches
Mistletoe, *Viscum*	Woodpigeon, thrushes, blackcap, tits, corvids, tree sparrow, finches, yellowhammer
Privet, *Ligustrum*	Pigeon, waxwing, thrushes (incl. robin), redstart, icterine + other warblers, tits, jay, finches
Rose, *Rosa*	Moorhen, pigeon, waxwing, thrushes, warblers, tits, red-backed shrike, corvids, finches (incl. serin + siskin)
Rowan, *Sorbus aucuparia*	Moorhen, green woodpecker, waxwing, thrushes (incl. robin), redstart, warblers, flycatcher, tits, nuthatch, jay, starling, house sparrow, finches
Sea buckthorn, *Hippophae*	Moorhen, common gull, waxwing, thrushes, warblers, corvids, starling, finches
Snowberry, *Symphoricarpos*	Waxwing, thrushes (incl. robin), warblers, tits, rook, finches
Spindle, *Euonymus*	Woodpigeon, waxwing, song thrush, robin, blackcap, garden warbler, tits (inc. long-tailed) corvids, sparrow, finches
Wayfaring tree et al, *Viburnum*	Pigeon, waxwing, thrushes (incl. robin), warblers, spotted flycatcher, corvids
Whitebeam, *Sorbus aria*	Black-headed gull, pigeon, waxwing, thrushes, blackcap, tits, corvids, starling, finches
Willow, *Salix*	Greylag goose, pigeon, waxwing, blackcap, tits (incl. marsh), jay, finches (incl. siskin + rosefinch)

OTHER NOTABLE TREES AND SHRUBS USED BY SEVERAL BIRD SPECIES

Ampelopsis hederacea

Bird cherry, *Prunus padus*

Broom, *Cytisus* spp.

Traveller's joy, etc., *Clematis* spp.

Conifers, Juniper

False acacia, *Robinia*

Hop, *Humulus*

Lilac, *Syringa*

Myrtle, *Myrtus*

Nettle tree, *Celtis*

Oleaster, *Elaeagnus*

Service tree, *Sorbus torminalis*

Stranvaesia, *Photinia*

Strawberry tree, *Arbutus*

Vine, *Smilax*

Virginia creeper, *Parthenocissus*

Wild cherry, *Prunus avium*

Yew, *Taxus baccata*

Yew (*Taxus baccata*)

CULTIVATED FRUITS ATTRACTING THE GREATEST VARIETY OF BIRDS

Apple (incl. crab)	Kestrel, pheasant, moorhen, woodpigeon, ring-necked parakeet, green woodpecker, skylark, waxwing, thrushes 6, blackcap, tits, treecreeper, golden oriole, corvids 5, sparrows 2, finches 9
Bilberry	Greylag goose, mallard, gulls 4, pigeon/dove 2, cuckoo, waxwing, warblers 6, willow tit, treecreeper, golden oriole, corvids 4, house sparrow, finches 6, reed bunting
Blackberry	Greylag goose, pheasant, moorhen, woodpigeon, waxwing, dunnock, thrushes 10, warblers 8, flycatchers, tits, nuthatch, golden oriole, corvids 4, starling, finches 7, yellowhammer
Cherry	Gulls 2, woodpigeon, woodpeckers 2, thrushes 8, warblers 4, flycatchers, tits, nuthatch, golden oriole, red-backed shrike, corvids 5, rose-coloured starling, tree sparrow, finches 5
Crowberry	Mallard, gulls 5, woodpigeon, meadow pipit, waxwing, dunnock, thrushes 3, spotted flycatcher, marsh + great tits, corvids 4, finches 4, yellowhammer
Currants	Pigeon/dove 2, woodpeckers 2, waxwing, thrushes 9, warblers 8, flycatchers 2, tits 2, golden oriole, corvids 2, sparrows 2, finches 5
Grape	Collared dove, ring-necked parakeet, bee-eater, roller, green woodpecker, waxwing, thrushes 5, warblers 2, golden oriole, corvids 5, starlings 2, sparrows 3, finches 3, yellowhammer
Mulberry	Pheasant, woodpigeon, waxwing, black redstart, warblers 4, spotted flycatcher, tits 2, nuthatch, golden oriole, corvids 5, rose-coloured starling, sparrows 2, finches 7
Pear	Moorhen, woodpeckers 2, skylark, waxwing, thrushes 6, warblers 4, tits 2, nuthatch, treecreeper, golden oriole, corvids 5, starling, sparrows 2, finches 6, corn bunting
Plum	Moorhen, pigeons 2, woodpeckers 2, waxwing, blackbird, warblers 4, tits 2, corvids 3, starling, sparrows 2, finches 3
Raspberry	Pheasant, woodpigeon, woodpeckers 2, waxwing, wren, thrushes 3, warblers 6, corvids 2, rose-coloured starling, hawfinch
Strawberry	Woodpigeon, waxwing, thrushes 7, blackcap, golden oriole, corvids 3, Spanish sparrow, finches 3

HERBACEOUS PLANTS PROVIDING FOOD FOR A LARGE VARIETY OF GARDEN BIRDS

Amaranthus	Dove, skylark, corvids, sparrows, finches, reed bunting
Aster, michaelmas daisy	Long-tailed tit, finches (incl. siskin + twite)
Bindweed, *Convolvulus*	Dove, warbler, sparrow, linnet
Bistort, *Persicaria*	Duck, goose, game, rail, coot, pigeon/dove, skylark, redstart, tit, corvid, starling, sparrow, finches, buntings
Burdock, *Arctium*	Geese, pigeon/dove, corvids, finches
Bur marigold, *Bidens*	Corvid, finches, bunting
Buttercup, celandine, *Ranunculus*	Duck, game, rail, moorhen, pigeon/dove, skylark, corvids, sparrows, finches, bunting
Chickweed, stitchwort, *Stellaria*	Goose, game, pigeon, wagtail, waxwing, rook, finches, buntings
Cinquefoil, *Potentilla*	Goose, pigeon, hoopoe, finches
Clover, *Trifolium*	Geese, partridge, gull, pigeon/dove, corvid, sparrows, finches
Cranesbill, *Geranium*	Dunnock, tits, sparrows, finches
Daisy, *Bellis*	Pigeon, finches
Dandelion, *Taraxacum*	Goose, pigeon/dove, tit, rook, starling, sparrow, finches 10, bunting
Dock, *Rumex*	Duck, moorhen, pigeon/dove, skylark, pipit, dunnock, redstart, jackdaw, finches 13, buntings
Evening primrose, *Oenothera*	Finches 10
Flax, *Linum*	Pigeon, pipit, sparrows, finches, bunting
Forget-me-not, *Myosotis*	Finches, bunting
Fumitory, *Fumaria*	Pigeon/doves, skylark, sparrow
Goosefoot, Good King Henry, *Chenopodium*	Goose, pheasant, pigeon/doves, skylark, pipit, dunnock, tit, rook, sparrows, finches, bunting
Groundsel, *Senecio*	Blackcap, finches, bunting
Hawkbit, *Leontodon*	Partridge, finches
Hemp-nettle, *Galeopsis*	Pigeon, tits, corvids, sparrow, finches
Knapweed, cornflower, *Centaurea*	Dove, tit, treecreeper, corvids, finches, bunting
Meadowsweet, *Filipendula*	Finches, bunting
Mugwort, *Artemisia*	Sparrow, finches, bunting
Nettle, *Urtica*	Pigeon, skylark, tit, jackdaw, sparrows, finches, buntings
Orache, *Atriplex*	Mallard, dove, corvids, finches, bunting
Plantain, *Plantago*	Pigeons, corvids, starling, sparrows, finches, buntings
Poppy, *Papaver*	Skylark, dunnock, tits, corvids, sparrows, finches
Primrose, cowslip, *Primula*	Pigeon/dove, waxwing, dunnock, tit, finches
Shepherd's purse, *Capsella*	Goose, pigeon, finches, bunting
Speedwell, *Veronica*	Pigeon/dove, skylark, finches
Spurge, *Euphorbia*	Pheasant, pigeon/doves, dunnock, jackdaw, sparrows, finches
Sunflower, *Helianthus*	Pigeon/doves, waxwing, tits, nuthatch, corvids, finches
Thistles, *Cirsium + Carduus*	Dunnock, warbler, tits, rook, finches
Vetch, *Vicia*	Pigeon/doves, corvids, starling, finch, bunting
Violet, pansy, *Viola*	Pigeon/doves, skylark, pipit, tits, rook, sparrows, finches
Willowherb, *Epilobium*	Dunnock, sparrow, finches, reed bunting
Wood sorrel, *Oxalis*	Pigeon, wren, tits, sparrow, finches
Yarrow, *Achillea*	Tits, sparrow, finches, bunting

NB: Families of birds listed in singular means only one species recorded for that plant. When listed in plural, indicates more than one species represented. Number after family indicates number of species. Pigeon/doves means one pigeon and several doves.

FURTHER NOTABLE HERBACEOUS PLANTS PROVIDING FOOD FOR GARDEN BIRDS

Aloe	Black redstart, garden warbler, blue tit, chaffinch
Arum	Robin, blackbird, whitethroat, garden warbler
Burnet, *Sanguisorba*	Greenfinch, goldfinch, linnet, redpoll
Campion, catchfly, *Silene*	Stock dove, starling, crossbill, rosefinch
Cat's ear, *Hypochaeris*	Greenfinch, goldfinch, siskin, linnet, twite
Chondrilla	Goldfinch, siskin, linnet, twite
Coltsfoot, *Tussilago*	Greenfinch, goldfinch, linnet, twite
Columbine, *Aquilegia*	Tits
Comfrey, *Symphytum*	Chaffinch, greenfinch, rosefinch
Deadnettle, *Lamium*	Willow tit, Spanish sparrow, brambling, linnet
Delphinium	Tits
Field scabious, *Knautia*	Greenfinch, goldfinch, linnet
Figwort, *Scrophularia*	Woodpigeon, meadow pipit, dunnock, chaffinch, bullfinch
Fritillaria	Nectar for garden warbler, blackcap
Golden rod, *Solidago*	Greenfinch, goldfinch, siskin, linnet, redpoll, twite
Hawksbeard, *Crepis*	Greenfinch, goldfinch, linnet, redpoll, reed bunting
Hawkweed, *Hieracium*	Greenfinch, goldfinch, siskin, linnet, redpoll, twite
Heaths, *Erica*	Meadow pipit, redwing, great tit, twite
Heathers, *Calluna*	Icterine warbler, bullfinch, crossbill
Iris	Blackbird, song thrush, blackcap
Lavender, *Lavandula*	Starling, serin, goldfinch, crossbill
Madder, *Rubia*	Turtle dove, redwing, garden warbler
Mallow, *Malva*	Woodpigeon, dunnock, house
Mignonette, *Reseda*	Turtle dove, house sparrows, bullfinch, twite
Pennycress, *Thlaspi*	Starling, serin, greenfinch, linnet, twite, reed bunting
Pimpernel, *Anagallis*	Stock dove, skylark, serin
Pinks, *Dianthus*	Skylark, dunnock, fieldfare, greenfinch
Scabious, *Scabiosa*	Marsh tit, goldfinch, linnet, bullfinch
Self-heal, *Prunella*	Willow tit, greenfinch, goldfinch, linnet, twite
Snapdragon, *Antirrhinum*	Blue tit, goldfinch, twite
St John's wort, *Hypericum*	Blackcap, twite, redpoll, bullfinch
Tansy, *Tanacetum*	Greenfinch, linnet, twite, redpoll
Teasel, *Dipsacus*	Chaffinch, goldfinch, crossbill
Thrift, *Armeria*	House sparrow, chaffinch, greenfinch, twite, crossbill

Comfrey (*Symphytum* sp.)

Lords and ladies/Cuckoo pint (*Arum maculatum*)

Maiden pink (*Dianthus deltoides*)

VEGETABLES AS A FOOD SOURCE

Asparagus	Waxwing, whitethroat, blackcap, jay, tree sparrow
Beans	Canada goose, pigeon/doves 3, whitethroat, corvids 3, hawfinch
Beet	Geese 2, red-legged partridge, chaffinch, greenfinch, linnet
Brassicas	Geese 2, pigeon/dove 4, meadow pipit, corvids 2, finches 6, reed + corn buntings
Carrots	Greylag goose, tree sparrow, twite
Capsicum	Carrion crow, rose-coloured starling
Chicory	Greenfinch, goldfinch, twite
Chickpea	Jackdaw
Cucumber, melon	Feral pigeon, magpie, rook, crow, house sparrow
Lettuce	Woodpigeon, serin, greenfinch, goldfinch, siskin, linnet
Peas	Geese 2, red-legged partridge, pigeon/dove 3, ring-necked parakeet, lesser whitethroat, blackcap, great tit, corvids 4, finches 6
Potato	Greylag goose, pigeon 2, waxwing, corvids 4
Radish	Pigeon 2, brambling, greenfinch, linnet, twite, redpoll, rosefinch, hawfinch
Turnip	Greylag goose, pigeon/dove 2, song thrush, crow, greenfinch, twite
Tomato	Feral pigeon

GRASSES, RUSHES AND SEDGES IMPORTANT AS FOOD SOURCES

Grasses

Barley, *Hordeum*

Maize, *Zea*

Millet, *Panicum*

Oat, *Avena*

Rye, *Secale*

Wheat, *Triticum*

Bents, *Agrostis*

Bristle grass, *Setaria*

Brome grass, *Bromus*

Cat's tail, *Phleum*

Cock's foot, *Dactylis*

Cockspur, *Echinochloa*

Cotton grass, *Eriophorum*

Couch grass, *Elymus (Agropyron)*

False oat grass, *Arrhenatherum*

Fescues, *Festuca*

Finger grass, *Digitaria*

Hair grass, *Aira*

Meadow foxtail, *Alopecurus*

Meadow grass, *Poa*

Purple moor grass, *Molinia*

Rye grasses, *Lolium*

Wavy hair grass, *Deschampsia*

Rushes and sedges

Rushes, *Juncus*

Woodrush, *Luzula*

Sedges, *Carex*

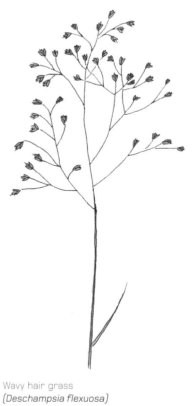

Wavy hair grass
(*Deschampsia flexuosa*)

Great woodrush (*Luzula sylvatica*)

The gardening techniques that will help attract birds to your garden are emphasized in this section. In small gardens, on balconies and patios, the complete choice of plants from trees to container plants is considered, as well as the need for weeds and water.

Gardening

GROWING ANNUALS, BIENNIALS AND PERENNIALS

Many plants, even forest trees, can be grown from seed. A good proportion of these will come true, with the seedlings having similar characteristics to the parents, while the attributes of others will vary. This is one of the cheapest methods of raising stock. Seeds should not be collected from the wild as many former common species are becoming scarce and are now protected by law.

Annuals

Annuals, because of their short life cycle (lasting less than a year), can easily be raised from seed. The same is true of biennials, which are sown one year and flower the next. Annuals and biennials are treated similarly.

Hardy annuals

Hardy annuals are usually sown where they are to flower. To prepare the bed beforehand, give it a fork over, remove the weeds and add a little compost. Finally, hoe the soil to a fine tilth. Sow the seed thinly in shallow drills or scatter it lightly over the prepared surface, then rake the area gently to ensure that most of the seed is covered slightly.

Seeds should be sown on moist, but not waterlogged, soil. They need water, warmth and air for germination; some are more exacting in their requirements than others. When conditions are reasonable, the seedlings should soon appear, usually in need of a little thinning. We prefer to wait and see the effects of pest damage (slugs)

before attempting to thin. Luckily, some plants are not susceptible to these attacks. Sowing times can be staggered, but the appearance of weed seedlings is a good indicator of when the soil conditions are suitable. Seed packets often give information on sowing requirements.

Half-hardy annuals

Half-hardy annuals cannot be sown outside until all frost danger has past. The majority of these seeds have their origins in warmer climates and need nurturing in the early stages. Seeds can be sown early in a fairly sandy compost in a seed tray, in modules (one or two seeds per module) or, if you are sowing only a few seeds, in a pot. They should be kept indoors on a windowsill, in a propagator, or in a frost-free conservatory or greenhouse. You should delay sowing half-hardy annuals in a cold greenhouse until the temperature has risen sufficiently and there is no danger of frosts affecting the germinating seedlings, which are extremely vulnerable.

When seedlings are large enough, they should be pricked out into seed trays, in a seedling compost, and placed in a light, frost-free position. After germination, seedlings in a pot or box soon become overcrowded and straggly as they struggle to reach the light. They also become prone to pests and disease. Damping-off and aphid infections spread quickly and can soon decimate a batch. If the seedlings are separated out as soon as they are large enough to handle and transplanted individually into pots or even a few per box, depending on the size of the species, they stand a much better chance of becoming sturdier, healthier plants.

(Opposite) Many annual and biennial plants can be grown from seed. The seedlings should be allowed to grow in individual pots.

Eventually, the seedlings will require hardening off. Hardening off is the method of preparing seedlings for planting outside by gradually introducing the pots and boxes to the cooler outside conditions. To do this, place them in a cold frame or a sheltered place for a few days. If frost threatens at night, they will need cover. When all frost danger is over, the seedlings can be planted out in open ground. If they have been thoroughly hardened off, they should not receive any setback. Plants removed straight from the greenhouse to the outside suffer shock. If this is severe, they may not recover; if it is less severe, they may turn blue with cold (like tomato plants) and so receive a setback to their growth.

Biennials

Biennials are useful flowers for attracting any early insects. Like foxglove and wallflowers, biennials are usually sown in shallow drills and transplanted into a nursery bed when they are large enough. The young plants are then finally moved to their flowering positions in the autumn. If there is room, they can be transplanted straight into their flowering positions.

BIRDWATCHER'S TIP
||||||||||||||||||||||||||||||||||||||||||||||||||||||||||||||||||||||||||||||||||||||||||||||||||||||

Half-hardy annuals, such as Tagetes, *French and African* marigolds, *Nemesia, Mesembryanthemums and zinnias are loved by bees, butterflies and other insects.*

Perennials

Some perennials are short-lived, others are not very hardy and unlikely to survive a cold, wet winter. Such perennials are often treated in the same way as half-hardy annuals, and with an early sowing can be induced to flower the same year. On seed packets they are often labelled as half-hardy annuals or half-hardy perennials to be treated like half-hardy annuals. Many are discarded after their first flowering. Pansies are often treated in this way, although many will survive for a second or third year.

The hardy, longer-lived perennials, such as aquilegias and delphiniums, can also be grown from seed, which is the cheapest method of producing a number of plants. However, there are a few drawbacks. Some, like lilies, take years to grow to flowering size. Others are notoriously difficult to germinate and require exacting conditions. Some gentians have a long dormancy period and require frost or cold to break it. Others have a double dormancy, which needs two spells of cold before germination will commence. Some set very little seed. The more tricky perennials require exacting growing conditions to thrive.

A further drawback is that seedlings may be inferior to the parents. Delphiniums, for example, do not breed true from seed, so if a named cultivar is required, it cannot be obtained from seed. If selected seed is grown, there is the potential for a new variety, but poorer specimens must be discarded. A packet of dwarf seeds will produce some plants that are not dwarf!

Some established perennial plants, including lilies, resent disturbance, but the majority, after several years, benefit from being divided into several sections which are then replanted. Primroses are best subdivided immediately after flowering has ceased or the plants lose their vigour. A little added compost helps as a booster.

A young delphinium spike grown from seed.

A dahlia's tubers should be dug up at the end of autumn and kept in a frost-free environment before planting out in spring.

STAKING

Staking is necessary for tall perennials, especially delphiniums: if they are left to grow too tall before staking, they are liable to snap in high wind or rain. Ideally, each spike should be staked. Another method, though more expensive, is to use ring-loops. In exposed regions some casualties can be expected. Some perennials are more resilient and so do not require staking.

Trussed-up plants look very unnatural: some of these should be left to sprawl. Invertebrates will congregate underneath sprawling plants in the damp, providing a food reserve for birds during a dry spell. Leaving a selection of seed heads will also provide bird food. When mature, some seed heads can be harvested for future use on the bird table and the rest left on the plant for birds to eat when required.

The smallest pieces can be potted up in a sandy cuttings compost until they are large enough to be planted out. If they have no roots, the base can be dipped in a little hormone rooting powder, planted and kept moist.

Cuttings from some plants, including pinks, carnations and fuchsias, will root readily in water: keep the water clean by adding a small piece of charcoal. When the roots are showing, the cuttings can be potted up. Cuttings can be grown in sandy compost in a pot.

When buying from a nursery or garden centre, ensure that the plants are healthy, that they are not infected by pests or diseases, and that they have no yellowing basal leaves due to being pot-bound. You can often take cuttings from these plants when you buy them and pot the cuttings up as a safeguard in case the original is lost.

Bulbs, corms and tubers

Some perennials survive the winter by using bulbs, corms and tubers. Hardy corms, like montbretia, can remain in the ground.

The corms increase vegetatively and so can be divided into separate clumps. Gladioli are less hardy and may not survive a winter in the ground. We dig our plants up and save the small cormlets around the base of the corm. The following spring we plant the large corms out in their flowering positions and the small cormlets in a shallow drill, being careful to keep the drill weed free to avoid confusion between gladiolus and grass shoots! The next year there are usually some cormlets large enough for flowering. Narcissi and tulip bulbs frequently have side offshoots that benefit from separation from the parent; these can also be used to increase the stock.

Dahlias and other tubers require frost-free storage, and must then be subdivided before being replanted in the spring. Each separated tuber should possess a growing shoot. These tubers can be planted in boxes and started into growth in a frost-free place, then planted out in the garden in late May, or when frosts are over.

SMALL TOWN GARDENS, BALCONIES AND PATIOS

Our front garden is small but it is densely packed with numerous plants. One tree and various shrubs and perennials surrounding a minute lawn are separated by a concrete driveway that covers nearly half the space leading out onto a busy city road. Despite this, we find a wide variety of birds frequent the garden, especially at quieter times of the day.

In springtime we have a female blackbird that regularly nests in a pretty, pink-flowering *Clematis montana* growing against the house. Blackbird, robin and song thrush routinely patrol the borders and lawn for morsels whilst dunnock and wren reappear from under the foliage from time to time in their hunt for food. Summer brings tits, dunnock, house sparrow and wren inspecting the brooms and roses for aphids. Autumn, and small parties of migrant goldcrests usually arrive in the brooms. These tiny birds seem oblivious to the passing pedestrians and traffic just a short distance away. Long-tailed tits, goldfinches and greenfinches fly from one tree to the next. In winter, brambling, siskin and redpoll pass through. Collared dove, jackdaw and starling perch on the chimney and TV aerial and a pied wagtail sometimes scuttles along the roofline. Overhead, kestrel and sparrowhawk can occasionally be seen and the summer swifts and sometimes swallows circle and flit by.

Some mammals also frequent our small front garden. These have included foxes, feral cats and bank voles. Once we watched a weasel scampering behind our low front wall and across the drive before disappearing through the hedge and into our neighbour's garden. Rabbits are about but so far, thankfully, they have remained outside the low wall.

And all this in a tiny front garden where no supplementary food or water is provided, and there are no nest boxes. This chapter suggests ways of adapting even the smallest spaces into bird-friendly areas.

Trees

Even in small gardens, wherever possible, plant at least one tree as this gives that third dimension of height. The tree will become a focal point in the vicinity, a lookout post and territorial marker – the natural entry point into the garden for birds. Avoid the large forest trees such as oak, ash and beech, which are clearly unsuitable, but if space allows, a silver birch with its attractive autumnal colours and peeling silvery bark will create only dappled shade in summer. The catkins and seed heads will provide an abundant source of food for many tits, siskins and redpolls over winter.

Other larger trees to consider in smaller gardens include hazel, osier and, in the south, field maple. In bygone days these trees were coppiced and pollarded; they can be cut back heavily when required.

An alternative is to grow hedging plants as natural trees. Good varieties include common hawthorn (*Crataegus monogyna*), the slightly smaller Midland thorn (*Crataegus laevigata*), blackthorn (*Prunus spinosa*), cherry plum (*Prunus cerasifera*), *Cotoneaster frigidus*, *C.* 'hybridus Pendulus', dogwood (*Cornus mas*), snowy mespilus (*Amelanchier canadensis*) and sea buckthorn (*Hippophae rhamnoides*). As these are hedging plants, they can be pruned regularly and kept to their allotted space. Many are thorny and provide safe nesting sites for some birds: the thorns act as a deterrent to larger predatory

Cotoneaser berries are much liked by blackbirds, thrushes and waxwings.

birds such as magpie, jackdaw and crow. Apple, crab apple, cherry, pear and plum are also good trees for birds and should not be neglected in a small garden. Growing trees on dwarfing rootstocks dramatically reduces the vigour of plants. Fruiting trees become a mecca for birds, often before humans have a chance to pick the fruit! Cherries attract all sorts, from the greedy guzzling blackbirds, great tits and nuthatches to woodmice and bank voles who remove the kernels from dropped cherry stones.

Columnar trained fruit trees and others grown on a dwarfing rootstock (see the table on page 97), have become readily available in recent years. These columnar trees, in varieties of apple, pear, cherry and plum, will grow to a maximum height of 6–8ft (1.8–2.5m) and are ideal for small spaces; they can even be grown successfully in large pots for the balcony and patio. Fruit bushes, red and white currants and gooseberries can also be grown successfully in pots.

Other trees suitable for small, confined spaces or for large pots include the corkscrew hazel (*Corylus contorta*) and Kilmarnock willow (*Salix caprea* 'Pendula') both of which are good insect plants. A third example is *Cotoneaster salicifolius* 'Pendulus'. This has bright red berries that are appreciated by blackbirds in autumn.

Climbers

Decades ago, only feral pigeon, starling and house sparrow thrived amongst the noise and pollution of the harsh, man-made landscapes of many towns and inner cities. Sadly, house sparrows are now scarce. However, tits (particularly blue tits), blackbirds and robins are doing well in this environment, and creating cover in town gardens for them and other birds will only encourage them further, providing them with a secure sanctuary.

Where there is little space for tall trees, climbing plants may be a suitable alternative, providing shelter and protection, roosting and nesting sites, which are so scarce in many manicured, formally laid-out town gardens (see the table on page 97). Common ivy (*Hedera helix*), being an evergreen, gives shelter throughout the winter to insects as well as birds and the berries become an important source of late winter nourishment. The variegated varieties of ivy are less vigorous growers and may be more suitable in restricted spaces. Climbing hydrangea (*Hydrangea petiolaris*) and Virginia creeper (*Parthenocissus quinquefolia*) are able to climb up walls without a trellis support, although they may need training in the early stages. They are both vigorous climbers and good plants for covering

In a garden, climbing plants can provide protection for birds.

The flowers of the honeysuckle plant are attractive to bees, and the berries are taken by many birds.

large, bare expanses of wall. By affixing trelliswork or supporting wires, other climbers can be grown: *Clematis* spp., honeysuckle (*Lonicera* spp.), winter jasmine (*Jasminum nudiflorum*), and wisteria (*Wisteria sinensis*). In a small-size garden avoid Russian vine (*Fallopia baldschuanica*, syn. *Polygonum baldschuanicum*), alternatively known as mile-a-minute plant, as it can grow 15ft (4.5m) or more each year.

Ivy (*Hedera helix*)

Lonicera hedge (*Lonicea nitida*)

Winter jasmine (*Jasminum nudiflorum*)

GARDEN CLIMBERS

Another rampant climber is our native clematis, also known as traveller's joy or old man's beard (Clematis vitalba). The finches and sparrows may devour the seed heads but it is too vigorous in a small, confined space. Other varieties of clematis are worthwhile: C. 'Jackmanii', C. 'Nelly Moser' and the yellow-flowering C. tangutica. However, they are fussy plants and require the right conditions to thrive. Ensure that their roots are shaded from direct sun: they must be kept cool as the plant is prone to wilt.

Honeysuckle should be grown in moisture-retentive soil. Never allow the roots to dry, as moist roots help the plant resist bad infestations of virus-spreading aphids. If unchecked, this virus may eventually kill the plant. Our native honeysuckle or woodbine (*Lonicera periclymenum*), produces bright red berries in autumn which, though harmful to humans, are beloved by birds. The nearest garden cultivars to this are *Lonicera periclymenum* 'Belgica' and 'Graham Thomas'.

Other berry plants, although not strictly climbers, can be trained up walls and are beneficial bird food plants. Firethorns (*Pyracantha atalantioides*, *P. coccinea* 'Lalandei',

P.c. 'Red Column', *P.* 'Orange Glow' and *P.* 'Saphyr Orange') have a profusion of tiny white starry flowers in June, followed by a mass of orange and red berries that disappear rapidly in autumn. Redcurrants (*Ribes sativum*) can also be trained in this way, the red, pearl-shaped fruits providing refreshing morsels of nourishment for many birds (and humans) during a dry July. Against low walls *Cotoneaster horizontalis* and *C. microphyllus* are effective and will provide an abundance of autumn berries.

Method for planting climbers

Plant climbers at an angle so that the roots grow away from the wall.

Dig a hole larger than the size of the plant's roots. Position the plant and infill with soil enriched with garden compost. Firm and water-in well.

Shrubs

Many of the shrubs mentioned in the previous chapters can grow well in a small garden. Shrubs are important as they provide shelter and protection for birds and for numerous insects further down the food chain. Many small town gardens lack suitable cover, roosting and nesting sites and, in consequence, are host to few birds. A few years ago in our front garden, a pair of goldfinches built their tiny feather nest in a forsythia bush next to the parked car in the drive. It was so close that they were continually disturbed – every time the car came in or out of the drive. With this disturbance, but probably due to the deluge of rain we had that summer, the birds deserted.

Forsythia (*Forsythia spectabilis*)

PRUNING CLIMBING PLANTS

With all climbing plants, it is important to prune them away from guttering and other external fixtures, such as aerials and satellite dishes, to prevent damage. Ivy in particular should always be kept in check by regular pruning and only grown up walls that are in good condition. If this is not done, the adventitious, self-clinging rootlets can damage the mortar in the stonework. If in doubt, choose an alternative climber and train the plant up trelliswork.

Cotoneaser (*Cotoneaster horizontalis*)

Container plants

For balconies, garden terraces and patios, berry plants might attract birds even when grown in large pots and containers. Our native bilberry (*Vaccinium myrtillus*), blueberry (*V. corymbosum*), cowberry (*V. vitis-idaea*), and prickly heath (*Gaultheria mucronata*) are good examples. They thrive in acid soils and should be grown in containers, even in large gardens, if the soil conditions are alkaline. In a shady corner *Aucuba japonica* will flourish. This plant has unusual, tiny, deep maroon, star-like flowers followed by red berries. *Hypericum* 'Orange Flair' has yellow flowers followed by red berries.

CARING FOR CONTAINER PLANTS

- There must be adequate drainage holes in the bottom of the container to prevent water-logging, which causes plants to rot.

- Cover the bottom with pieces of old crock or pieces of broken polystyrene. The latter will reduce the overall weight of the container – an important consideration if containers are to be placed on balconies or used for roof gardens.

- Preferably, plant shrubs and trees in a peat-free compost mixture, leaving a rim of at least 1½–2in (40–50mm) from the top of the pot for ease of watering. Do not use the modern composts that have insecticide added: if there are no insects in the soil and on the plants, there is less food for birds.

- Make sure that you water the plants well and continue watering throughout the year when necessary. Plants in pots and containers dry out faster than those in open soil. Special care is needed during the drier months.

- Trees, shrubs and other plants may require regular feeding during the growing season.

- Pots and containers placed against a wall or balcony should be turned round slightly every week to prevent lopsided growth.

- Bring plants inside in winter or wrap a thick layer of hessian or bubble wrap around the pot and stand it in a sheltered position. This will insulate the plant's roots from damaging frosts.

Skimmias can be successfully grown in pots, but a male (*S. rubella*) and female (*S. veitchii*) plant may be needed if they are to set berries, and the red berries do not seem to be so attractive to birds. I have only seen an immature blackbird and an oversized woodpigeon try to feed on them, the weight of the latter causing some disfiguration to the plant in the pot!

Container-grown
Skimmia with berries.

Flowering plants

In every birdwatcher's garden, whatever the size, there must be a space for a few flowering plants. In addition to their foliage providing essential cover, the flowers will attract insects. This is a necessary component of many birds' diet, together with the nectar and seed heads of a variety of garden annual, biennial and perennial plants.

In the confined space of a small town garden, fewer of these plants can be grown, so the choice becomes vital. Where possible, try to ensure that some plants are in flower throughout the year, or at least from early spring through to autumn. Although it is good horticultural practice, avoid deadheading the flowers. Removing the fading blooms may encourage more flowers but it will deprive the birds of the seeds.

Annuals

Annuals to consider include love-in-the-mist (*Nigella*), cornflower (*Centaurea*), love-lies-bleeding (*Amaranthus*), mignonette (*Reseda odorata*), pansy (*Viola*), poached egg plant (*Limnanthes douglasii*), poppy (*Papaver* spp.; *P. rhoeas*, single 'Shirley' series is the nearest to our native flower) and sunflowers (*Helianthus annuus*).

SUNFLOWERS

||||||||||||||||||||||||||||||||||||||||||||||||||||||||||||||||||||||||||||||||||||||

Sunflower 'Pacino' and 'Teddy Bear' are dwarf varieties and will thrive equally well grown in pots and tubs against a sunny wall on the patio or balcony. When mature, the seed heads of these can be dried and stored, to be put out for the birds in deep winter when food is scarce. The Helianthus Annuus shown here is a tall, fast-growing variety suitable for small gardens.

Poppy seed head

Biennials

Biennials such as forget-me-not (*Myosotis*), foxglove (*Digitalis*), honesty (*Lunaria*) and wallflowers (*Cheiranthus cheiri*) do not die down during the first winter and thus provide cover for sheltering insects which, in turn, makes them haunts for wren and dunnock. In springtime in our garden, green-veined white and orange tip butterflies are attracted to the honesty flowers and one particular house sparrow seems to relish plucking off the purple petals, one by one!

Perennials

Low-growing perennials or rockery plants, such as *Alyssum*, *Arabis*, *Aubrieta*, *Lithodora*, London pride (*Saxifraga urbium*), soapwort/tumbling Ted (*Saponaria ocymoides*) and thrift (*Armeria*), require a warm, dry, sunny site and are ideal for growing in rockeries, cracks in the paving around the edge of a patio, or cascading out of tubs and containers. These spring-flowering plants attract early bees, butterflies and many other insects to the garden and, in turn, higher up the food chain, dunnock and wren creep about the foliage seeking nourishment.

For semi-shaded sites choose Solomon's seal (*Polygonatum*), red campion (*Silene dioica*) and bluebells (*Hyacinthoides non-scripta*), or the Spanish bluebell (*H. hispanica*). Ferns will grow in shady areas, providing plenty of cover, and sparrows enjoy nibbling at the young spores in late summer.

In a sunny border, try meadow cranesbill (*Geranium pratense*), corn cockle (*Agrostemma githago*), corn marigold (*Chrysanthemum segatum*), field scabious (*Knautia arvensis*), common knapweed (*Centaurea nigra*), wild pansy (*Viola tricolor*) and wild strawberry (*Fragaria vesca*). The tiny, juicy, red strawberries that fruit in the heat of summer are beloved by many birds and mammals.

Pot-grown perennial plants, including wildflowers, are best planted out in early autumn so that the roots have time to establish before the growing season of the following year. If this is not possible, plant in March or April.

Honesty (*Lunaria*) is a biennial plant. It is easy to grow in almost any soil and requires little maintenance.

(Below) Tumbling Ted (*Saponaria ocymoides*) is a spreading perennial that covers the ground, and does well in chalky or dry soils. It has abundant pink flowers in the spring.

(Above) *Lithodora diffusa* 'Heavenly Blue' (syn. *Lithospermum*) is a low-growing perennial plant with bright blue flowers. It is ideal for a rockery and and lasts throughout the summer.

BIRDWATCHER'S TIP

If space permits, try growing a few larger perennials. (A detailed selection of herbaceous plants, perennials, annuals and wildflowers can be found on pages 74–75.) These, interspersed with some native wildflowers, may attract a greater variety of wildlife.

Weeds

A birdwatcher's garden is not an immaculate and tidy garden. Allowing a few common weeds to seed will be beneficial to birds. We have watched brightly-coloured goldfinches in our garden nibbling at the heart-shaped seed cases of shepherd's purse. They will also feed on dandelions, coltsfoot, hawksbeard and self-heal amongst other common weed seeds. House sparrows will eat all manner of weeds and seeds, including the leaves of willowherb and tufted vetch. Nettles are also beneficial to butterflies, in addition to providing food for buntings, finches and sparrows. Nettles are the food plant for peacock, red admiral and small tortoiseshell caterpillars.

Great tits are mainly insectivores. They have been known to reduce caterpillar populations in apple orchards.

WINTER PLANTS

As mentioned before, winter is a difficult time for birds. An autumnal tidy up will deprive birds of valuable seeds and insect food and would be better left until the following spring.

Tubs, windowboxes and containers can be planted with winter-flowering pansies or violas and a miniature ivy. Chaffinch, greenfinch, coal tit and house sparrow may come and devour the seed heads, whilst the robin and blackbird may poke about in the soil of a windowbox for morsels, especially if the soil elsewhere is frozen. We have often watched a robin routinely rummage through the small plant pots up against our house, and sparrows seem to peck at anything that is growing; some birds will take advantage whatever their surroundings.

Primroses (*Primula vulgaris*) and the other garden cultivars are also good plants for a winter tub or window box. The seeds of these cultivars are eaten by chaffinch, greenfinch, great tit and dunnock, amongst others, whilst the yellow flowers seem to be mysteriously shredded by blackbird and house sparrow.

Lawns

In a small town garden there is not enough space to cultivate a spring meadow or a summer hay meadow (see Chapter 4, pages 136 and 137), which, in any case, would look unsightly to the neighbours. In their place, natural lawns regularly mown provide a good habitat for certain birds, especially if a few native flowers are allowed to grow, as these will attract insects.

Lawns are particularly preferable to Mediterranean-style, low-maintenance gravel gardens. These are hot and dry with exotic flowering plants and any native weeds are suppressed beneath layers of membrane and gravel. This produces an alien environment for birds where few insects and natural seeds are available. Because of this, such gardens attract very few visiting birds.

To increase the range of foods provided, you can incorporate a few low-growing plants into the lawn. Examples include bird's-foot trefoil (*Lotus corniculatus*), clover (*Trifolium pratense*), daisy (*Bellis perennis*), self-heal (*Prunella vulgaris*), Germander speedwell (*Veronica chamaedrys*) and wild thyme (*Thymus serpyllum*). (A more complete list can be found in Chapter 4.)

NEST BOXES

Natural holes in ancient trees and thick rambling hedgerows are at a premium in small town gardens and you may need to supplement what is available. The most suitable alternative is to erect a nest box on a tree or fence, or even against a wall of the house. Nest boxes for birds such as blue tits and robins not only provide a safe site for raising young but may also be used as roosting sites over the winter. For this reason, do not remove them after the breeding season. (A more detailed account of nest boxes can be found in Chapter 4.)

Food

Wherever you live, and whatever size of garden you have, from window ledge to tiny back yard, the most successful way to attract birds is to provide food. A regular supply of food can attract all manner of birds, even in the heart of towns and cities. Depending on the location, sparrows, pigeons, starlings and gulls may be attracted. By providing peanuts, scarcer birds, such as blue tit, great tit and greenfinch, may find their way through the most built-up areas.

In winter, harsh conditions drive many more birds from the surrounding countryside into urban areas in search of shelter and food. The most surprising birds can be found in the most peculiar places. We remember one severe winter when the river was frozen, seeing two desperate grey wagtails flitting about the entrance of the chemist's in the market place looking for morsels amongst the paving stones. This was at 10 o'clock in the morning and all the shoppers and traffic were about. By providing a regular supply of food, anything might come.

Rooftops and high balconies might not attract such a diverse range of birds, but providing food may entice pied wagtail, crows, jackdaws and rooks, black-headed and herring gulls, blackbird, house sparrows and starlings, collared dove, feral pigeon and woodpigeon, amongst a few others.

Nowadays there are peanut holders, seed trays and water holders that have been specially designed to adhere to windows by means of two suction pads. Surprisingly, these are able to take a great deal of weight. Two collared doves come up to our window to feed from the seed tray we have placed there, and even with two of these great greedy guzzlers perched side by side it did not slip! One precaution; we have noticed that peanuts leave a greasy residue on the window around the holder and in damp weather this causes the suction pads to slip and occasionally to fall off. Clean the window regularly to prevent this happening. Here, many birds are encouraged to the window: sparrows, finches, blackbird and robin, tits and even nuthatch have all come to the holder to hammer at the peanuts.

Water

Another necessity is water. Even in a small town garden or balcony, providing water for drinking and bathing might entice birds that otherwise would not come. Any simple container will suffice, whatever its size. It need not necessarily be some grand, ornate sculpture – an upturned dustbin lid dug into the ground or a shallow plastic bowl both make adequate birdbaths.

We have set an old frying pan into an old raised trough just outside our kitchen window, placing a stone in the bottom of the pan so that the water is not too deep for the smaller birds. Birds that come to drink include gregarious sparrows, two collared doves, greenfinch and chaffinches, blue and coal tits, dunnock, blackbirds and the odd starling – surprisingly, an uncommon bird in our neighbourhood.

Peanuts may attract blue tits to more built-up areas.

DWARFING ROOTSTOCKS FOR FRUIT TREES

(Suitable for growing in large pots and small spaces)

Trees	Rootstocks
Apples	M9, M27, M26 *
Pears	Quince 'C'
Damsons Gages Plums	Pixy *
Cherries	Inmil * Damil *

* For columnar trained trees

SELECTED CLIMBERS TO PROVIDE COVER AND SHELTER FOR BIRDS

Clematis (*Clematis* spp.)	Evergreen and deciduous. White, pink through to deep purple flowers.
Climbing hydrangea (*Hydrangea petiolaris*)	Deciduous. Pretty, white, lace-cap flowers. Vigorous grower but suitable for north-facing wall.
Common ivy (*Hedera helix*)	Evergreen. Tiny, nondescript green flowers in September/November, followed by black berries in late winter. Food for thrushes and pigeons.
Firethorn (*Pyracantha* spp.)	Evergreen. Red-berried varieties preferable to birds such as song thrush, blackbird, starling, blackcap, greenfinch and waxwing.
Honeysuckle (*Lonicera periclymenum* var.)	Deciduous and evergreen. Pink and cream tubular flowers. Red berries eaten by finches, thrushes and warblers.
Virginia creeper (*Parthenocissus quinquefolia*)	Deciduous. Rich autumn colour. Food plant for blackcap, redpoll, spotted flycatcher and magpie, among others.
Winter jasmine (*Jasminum nudiflorum*)	Deciduous. Bright yellow flowers from December to March.
Wisteria (*Wisteria sinensis*)	Deciduous. Vigorous climber with racemes of blue, pea-like flowers in May/June.

The natural garden can be enhanced, making it more desirable to local birdlife, by installing bird tables, hanging feeders and nest boxes – carefully constructed and sited for best effect. A pond, birdbath or bog garden will also be greatly appreciated.

Man-made provisions

SUPPLEMENTARY AIDS TO FEEDING

Even a well-stocked garden, with berried trees and shrubs, seeding annuals and perennials, a good lawn and readily available water, requires some supplements to assist birds in an increasingly difficult environment: natural foods are becoming scarcer. Birds benefit considerably when additional foods are supplied regularly.

Feeding habits

The feeding habits of birds are variable. Some species, including gulls, feed in open spaces, whereas others require the shelter of a hedge or shrubs. If there are cats about, an open site is a better option – unless a sparrowhawk can swoop down before its intended quarry can reach the safety of shelter. Rooftops are designated as open spaces by the British Trust for Ornithology.

Other species prefer a raised bird table, either suspended or on a post. These are best placed a little away from cover to prevent cats from jumping onto unsuspecting victims. There are many types of standard bird table, ranging from a shallow tray to various roofed varieties. Some are even squirrelproof, and hanging feeders can be attached to these.

Another preference of many birds is to eat from feeders, open or closed, that are fixed to a window (by suckers) or placed on a windowsill. Open trays can be used for seed and/or water and closed wire containers for peanuts. Both types enable excellent close-up views of birds feeding.

Many birds use several feeding methods. The song thrush is reputed to be a ground feeder, but if hungry they can be seen devouring the food placed on a bird table – until the more aggressive male blackbird arrives, that is. Dunnocks behave similarly. We have seen tits not only hanging on nut and seed feeders, but also on the ground, at bird tables and at the window. Grey and pied wagtails will devour fragments of bread at our table in hard weather. Other birds we've seen feeding from a hanging wire peanut holder include chaffinch, brambling, robin and long-tailed tit.

Jackdaws have appeared at our bird tables over the last few years and rather dominate the scene, devouring large quantities of food; sadly, smaller birds do not have much of a chance. The jackdaws, mainly in pairs, roam the neighbourhood looking for food. Their numbers have increased considerably since the advent of central heating, which allows them to use chimneys for nesting. They readily consume food thrown out on the ground and will squabble to reach it if food is placed on a bird table. They will even eat smaller seed, using a scooping technique with their head on one side. One pair regularly try for the peanuts in our hanging feeder. Sometimes they wrench the lid open, whilst at other times one bird clings to the cage, swinging precariously, and pecks out the nuts while its mate waits for the fragments to fall!

Many birds are antagonistic when feeding; some individual robins and blackbirds notoriously so. One male siskin showed outstanding behaviour on a close encounter. He would display aggressively even at greenfinches when they

---

BIRDWATCHER'S TIP
||||||||||||||||||||||||||||||||||||||||||||||||||||||||||||||||||||||||||||||||||||

Only moderate amounts of supplementary foods should be given at any one time, to avoid attracting vermin. Remember that bird feeding stations should be cleaned regularly to prevent the build-up of bacterial disease, like salmonella.

decided to have a turn at the nuts. He won every contest! Once, one of us went to replace the peanut supply, thinking no birds were present, and were just about to open the top of the feeder when suddenly it swung round and the siskin's head came into view. His aggressive behaviour took over and immediately he displayed, with wings outstretched, looking larger than life. He made some very loud and long hissing sounds. Not wishing him to depart, I retreated to the sound of his hiss! No other visiting siskin has

behaved quite so aggressively; they mostly give way to the greenfinches or the sparrow brigade. Siskins, like redpolls, prefer to remain on natural foods until the supply runs low.

BIRDWATCHER'S TIP

Do not put grapes, currants, raisins, sultanas or fruit cake out for the birds if you have a dog. If ingested, even in relatively small amounts, these fruits can be fatal to dogs.

This is a well-sited bird table, being close to a natural habitat, providing shelter and giving a variety of food both on the table and in the hanging feeder.

The coal tit is a regular visitor to bird feeders, where it will pick up nuts and seeds and hide them for later. Unfortunately, the coal tit often forgets where it left its store!

Supplementary winter feeding helps small birds when food is hard to find or buried under snow.

Peanut extraction

A peanut cage that can be attached to a window will offer some wonderful opportunities for the close viewing of birds and the different methods they use for obtaining food. The same applies to open window feeders.

Different birds have varying methods of extracting peanuts. The blue tit arrives and hammers fast, with a quiet tapping sound, but the great tit puts a great deal of effort into hammering, resulting in loud bangs with longer intervals. Nearly every time the great tit hammers it extracts a small piece of nut and uses its tongue to take the bits speedily inside its beak.

The coal tit flies onto the feeder only when no other bird is present. It is faster than the blue tit at pecking, and feeds with speedy yet gentle taps until a sparrow or other bird appears, when it quickly flies away.

When the house sparrow arrives, as well as trying to hammer the peanuts out of the cage, it also grinds away with its beak so that the wire mesh holding the nuts is filed down and the protective coating is worn away. It makes sounds of rubbing, grinding and hammering.

Greenfinches are even more vigorous in grinding and chewing; whilst the siskin quietly chews and occasionally twists its head upwards to view the situation whilst eating.

Woodpeckers have not been so near our house, but their forceful hammering, using special neck and back muscles, is well documented. It is felt that they could crack any window with their forceful vibrations!

Food scraps

In some gardens, large scraps of food, even whole slices of toast or crusts, are thrown out for birds. If this is done on a regular basis, the corvid population (of carrion crows, magpies and jackdaws) sits around waiting at all nearby vantage points – trees, posts and rooftops. In winter their numbers are swelled by circling black-headed and herring gulls. One garden's count revealed six carrion crows, six magpies, at least 30 jackdaws and over 30 gulls! When chunky food is thrown out, the largest birds swoop down, squabbling and grabbing food, and then fly away. Frequently, crusts are dropped and not retrieved. The unfortunate consequences of throwing out large quantities of food is that any leftovers attract undesirable pests. These can be a nuisance to the neighbours.

Some years ago, after every tea break in a certain university department, the caterer used to throw out the crumbs from biscuit tins onto a rooftop balcony. A large gathering of birds, mainly herring and black-headed gulls, jackdaws and sparrows, used to wait on the rooftop for the repast. As time went on, one impatient herring gull would come to the glass door and hammer loudly with his beak to indicate that he was waiting! This

BIRDWATCHER'S TIP

The siting of feeders is important. The most preferable position is one that is subject to the least disturbance. Our feeders are on the window nearest a hedge, away from the sparrowhawk route through our garden. Most species that come into the garden for supplementary foods will also come to this quiet corner to feed.

behaviour is not limited to gulls: there are many instances of birds tapping on windows or going indoors every day for their rations.

In severe weather, birds need to know when and where there will be food without having to waste valuable energy hunting for it. This makes supplementary feeding an extremely important factor in their survival.

NUTHATCH

Nuthatches hammer vigorously when attacking nuts. They use their whole body, sometimes even flapping their wings. They eat small pieces of nut in situ but take whole nuts or large pieces away to the nearby hedge or tree. Here they lodge the nut in a crack on a bough and hammer further. From indoors, the noise made by the nuthatch is the loudest.

Bird tables

Every birdwatcher's garden must have a bird table. Bird tables come in all manner of shapes, sizes and designs, from very cheap plastic trays to folksy rustic tables. Avoid nest box tables, a combination that will create territorial conflict. Any birds using the nest box will be continually disturbed by the birds feeding below.

Simple seed trays can be made using a flat, rectangular piece of wood at least 18 x 12in (450 x 300mm). The exact measurements do not matter, but the wood should be at least $1/2$–$3/4$in (15–20mm) thick. To this, attach a thin strip of wood, $3/4$–$1^1/4$in (20–30mm) in height, along each side, leaving small gaps at the corners. The lip will prevent the seed blowing away in windy weather and the gaps will help with cleaning and drainage. This simple seed tray can be mounted on a pole 3ft (1m) above the ground, attached to a trellis, wall or windowsill, or suspended from the branch of a tree.

The addition of a roof will prevent the foodstuffs left on the table from turning into soggy porridge in wet weather. It may also deter larger birds, though in our garden the roof does not seem to prevent the eight or nine jackdaws swooping in and raiding all the food! Even a fat woodpigeon managed the complicated manoeuvre from the roof to the tray below. Once there, the pigeon stayed for some considerable time, but it was companionable enough to allow a collared dove to join it.

(Opposite) This unusual bird table can be attached to the outside of a window, attracting a good view of garden visitors.

(Left) A regular supply of food on a bird table is needed, especially during the cold winter months.

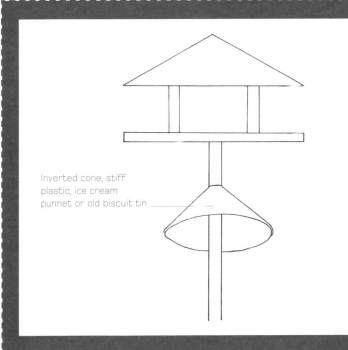

Inverted cone, stiff
plastic, ice cream
punnet or old biscuit tin

UNWANTED VISITORS

If a garden is plagued with either rats or grey squirrels, invert a firm ice cream carton or biscuit tin on the pole beneath the bird table as shown left. Don't place the table too near a hedge or tree or the roof of a low building as both of these creatures, as well as cats, are capable of climbing and jumping a considerable distance.

Hanging feeders

Hanging receptacles represent a third method of feeding. Although these swing in the wind and can therefore spill some seed if there is a high wind, their great advantage is that they give smaller birds more chances to obtain supplementary food, as only a few large birds will attempt to reach food in a hanging feeder. One example in our garden is a jackdaw, which regularly hangs onto a feeder to extract peanuts. His mate waits on the ground below to pick up any dropped fragments. Seven or eight other jackdaws visit but only try for food on the ground or on the bird table. They rapidly demolish the food on the bird table, leaving little for any other visitors.

Long-tailed tits hang together on the peanut cage – only occasionally has a single bird paid a fleeting visit to the table. Tits, sparrows,

(Above) Hanging peanut holders give smaller birds a chance to get food.

(Left) Larger birds such as pigeons can scare away tiny birds from collecting food. Help smaller birds by using hanging bird feeders.

finches, even chaffinch, brambling, nuthatch and a robin, all hang on the wire mesh holder. Even more finches visit the plastic holder with perches. Bear in mind that one large predator that can easily devastate a hanging feeder is the grey squirrel.

Hanging feeders are especially suitable for peanuts and large seeds such as sunflowers, as the small mesh size prevents small birds from taking away a whole nut. If a nestling or youngster is fed a whole nut, it may choke and be unable to swallow or breathe. Plastic hanging containers are suitable for the smaller bird seed, as they have just a few small holes above lips or perches. These holes are usually at the base, though some feeders may have one or two holes further up the cylinder. Thin, plastic mesh bags are of no use for small seeds and are easily ripped open by greenfinches when used to hold peanuts. Coconut halves and fat are other food items that can be hung from a branch or table.

We have never seen any preference shown towards yellow or red plastic net holders for peanuts, and for many years siskins have fed from white or dark metal cages.

Blue tits will be attracted to almost any garden with a bird feeder, usually giving acrobatic performances when feeding.

(Left) Hanging 'lantern' with sunflower seeds.

Supplementary foods

Peanuts

These should only be obtained from sources guaranteeing that the nuts are aflotoxin free. If there is any contamination, the mould, which is lethal for birds, will spread quickly throughout the supply. The larger Chinese nuts are more expensive than the Indian or Vietnamese varieties, but if they are labelled 'safe' then they are acceptable. Salted peanuts should not be given to birds. Salty foods generally are not suitable for birds, as they cause dehydration and can severely harm their digestive systems.

Peanuts, like beech nuts, are particularly rich in oils and protein, and the peanut granule is a very concentrated source. For this reason, only small quantities should be given. Hedgehogs like them and rodents will sniff out leftovers!

Peanuts in shells can be strung and hung from a branch. Years ago we had a queue of blue tits after these nuts, clinging to the string and extracting the kernels. Now, only occasionally does a tit try for these hanging nuts; most prefer the easy access of those already shelled.

Sunflower seeds

These seeds, used in margarine manufacture, are rich in oils. A number of varieties are sold, and birds seem to consume them all equally well. Of the husks that are left behind, the black varieties are not so conspicuous as the cheaper striped and larger seeds. More expensive still are sunflower hearts, which are seeds without their husks. As sunflower hearts are high-energy foods they should only be given in small quantities.

Peanut granules

Wild bird seed

Flaked maize

Sunflower hearts

Millet

Songster food

Wild bird food

This varies enormously: each distributor has a different seed mixture. Cheaper mixtures usually contain a high percentage of cereal with little variety, appealing mainly to sparrows, doves and pigeons. A greater variety of birds are attracted to mixes containing a good percentage of millet, peanut granules, pinhead oatmeal, flaked maize, sunflower and other seeds. Other high-energy seeds often found include hemp, linseed and rape.

Table and feeder seed are variants: the latter contains no maize so that it can flow easily through a feeder. Songster food formulas are especially suitable for birds with fine bills, but jackdaws also like it!

Finch food, canary seed and millet are enjoyed by finches and sparrows and appreciated by tits, dunnock, robin, wren and blackbird.

Niger seed

Pinhead oatmeal

Pinhead oatmeal

This excellent constituent of mixed bird seed can also be bought separately. The first time we placed some on our bird table, adjacent to niger and other bird seed, a collared dove arrived and sat on the roof, seemingly contemplating the food. Eventually it flew onto the table and, ignoring the other seeds, took a few mouthfuls of oatmeal, paused, then settled to eat it in earnest. The next bird, a jackdaw, had to turn its head onto one side to scoop the oatmeal up with its beak. Oatmeal also appears popular with other species.

Niger seed

These small, shiny, black *Compositae* seeds are another food that is rich in oil. Although they are supposed to attract a wide variety of birds, and to be a particular favourite of goldfinches, we have not managed to attract a single goldfinch to them so far! We have tried it at different times of the year, and various RSPB local group members have tried samples – in every case other bird seed was preferred. Many birds ignored it, and while a few individuals tried sampling it, these were notable exceptions. Only chaffinch returned for more. At present, niger does not appear to be very popular in our area of County Durham, but possibly it is elsewhere. Again, if nothing else is available, then birds will eat it.

Corn and wheat mixtures

Cereal mixtures are liked by ground-feeding game birds, ducks, pigeons, doves and sparrows but less appreciated by the finer-beaked finches. Oyster grit is sometimes added to these mixtures to give a much-needed calcium supply.

Household supplementary foods

The list of possible foods is enormous. Further examples are provided in the table on page 115. Whether these are eaten depends greatly on the availability of alternatives. Some individuals within a species will show different preferences from the rest.

Bread, cake and biscuits

Bread, white or brown, as breadcrumbs or crusts, is about the most distributed food for birds. Cake and biscuit crumbs are also devoured. Many householders throw out the ends of loaves for birds, but these can attract unwanted visitors. Small fragments of bread or breadcrumbs are better, as they allow a much greater variety of birds to partake of the food. Smaller birds with fine beaks will only tackle large pieces of bread if desperate. Corvids and gulls will seize a large piece of bread and carry it away but often drop it and leave it where it falls. These neglected crumbs can then encourage unwanted vermin.

Stale bread needs to be moistened to prevent it being detrimental to young or starving birds. If dry bread is eaten it will swell up in the bird's stomach leaving it feeling replete and unable to take in any more food. The result of this is that young or starving birds will become undernourished, unable to feed again until the bread has been digested, when it may be too late for more food. If food is scarce in winter, or a nestling is not fed sufficiently, the bird will die.

Fats

Suet, either hanging or flaked on a bird table, is a much-liked fat source. A bird cake can be made by using either suet or dripping as a base and adding other ingredients, such as wild bird seed, sunflower seed, breadcrumbs, scraps and dried fruit. When the cake is cold, place pieces on a bird table or in a hanging receptacle.

Break bread for birds into small fragments and moisten it slightly.

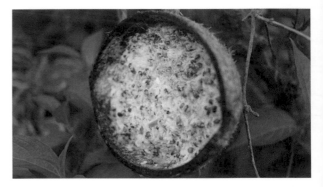
A mixture of melted fat and bird food, allowed to set in halved coconut shells, is welcomed by many birds in the cold months.

Blackbirds readily come to garden feeding stations.

Bacon, cheese and other fatty foods

These high-energy foods may be hung or placed on a bird table. Even song thrush, woodpeckers and long-tailed tit appreciate them. Fat smeared on a tree trunk may even attract a treecreeper.

Apples, pears and dried fruit

Some species will only eat fresh fruit whilst it is still on the tree, but many relish apples and pears when they are thrown out on the ground, especially during cold, snowy conditions. At such times, redwing, fieldfare, blackcap, and other members of the thrush family are eager to demolish them. An aggressive blackbird will spend a lot of time and energy chasing away other birds, even chaffinches!

Dried fruit, raisins and sultanas are consumed by quite a variety of species and are a welcome addition to the bird table.

Potato: mashed, roast or baked

Another popular leftover that is thrown out for birds is potato. We only throw potato out in winter. Then the demolition squad of jackdaws descends, taking away great beakfuls and returning for more. Any remaining scraps are eaten by blackbird, blue tit, nuthatch, finches and house sparrow.

Kitchen scraps

These, by definition, are highly variable, so quite a variety of birds consume them. During bad weather, even heron, moorhen and kestrel will come into gardens in search of food. Remember that salted food should not be given.

Mealworms and waxworms

Insectivorous birds, including robin, wren, dunnock, woodpecker, tits and sparrows, will eat these live foods. Unfortunately, these foods have a short life span so they need to be used quickly.

Baked potato is a leftover that is suitable for garden birds.

Coconuts

This is another food that is especially appreciated by tits in winter. Coconuts should be halved and have the milk drained before being hung from a branch. Desiccated coconut should never be used: it is disastrous for birds. Because it swells up inside their bodies, they become unable to eat enough food to survive.

SUPPLEMENTARY FOOD TABLES

The tables on pages 112–113 give just an indication of some of the food eaten by birds; these observations are based mainly in northeast England. They also indicate some feeding preferences, as several different foods were made available simultaneously.

The 26 species listed in these tables regularly feed on supplementary foods in gardens. There are over 80 species that will eat these foods either daily or occasionally (examples are listed on page 114). Many species only seek supplementary food in extreme weather conditions when their diet becomes very different from normal; for example, a lesser whitethroat has been recorded as eating suet.

COMMERCIAL SUPPLEMENTARY FOODS FOR BIRDS

	Peanuts	Peanut granules	Sunflower seeds	Wild bird seed	Songster food	Millet	Flaked maize	Pinhead oatmeal	Corn/wheat	Niger
Pheasant				✓					✓	
Woodpigeon	✓			✓		✓	✓	✓	✓	
Collared dove	✓	✓	✓	✓	✓	✓	✓	✓	✓	✓
Great spotted woodpecker	✓			✓						
Wren		✓		✓	✓	✓		✓		
Dunnock	✓	✓	✓	✓	✓	✓	✓	✓	✓	✓
Robin	✓	✓	✓	✓	✓	✓	✓	✓		✓
Blackbird	✓	✓		✓	✓	✓	✓	✓		
Song thrush		✓	✓	✓	✓	✓		✓		✓
Redwing		✓		✓						
Blackcap	✓	✓	✓	✓						
Long-tailed tit	✓	✓								
Marsh tit	✓		✓	✓						
Coal tit	✓	✓	✓	✓	✓	✓	✓	✓		
Blue tit	✓	✓	✓	✓	✓	✓	✓	✓		
Great tit	✓	✓	✓	✓	✓		✓			
Nuthatch	✓	✓	✓	✓	✓		✓	✓		
Magpie	✓			✓						
Jackdaw	✓	✓	✓	✓	✓	✓	✓	✓	✓	✓
Starling	✓	✓	✓	✓	✓	✓	✓	✓	✓	
House sparrow	✓	✓	✓	✓	✓	✓	✓	✓	✓	✓
Chaffinch	✓	✓	✓	✓	✓	✓	✓	✓	✓	✓
Brambling	✓	✓	✓	✓		✓		✓		✓
Greenfinch	✓	✓	✓	✓	✓	✓			✓	✓
Goldfinch	✓		✓	✓		✓				✓
Siskin	✓		✓					✓		✓

HOUSEHOLD SUPPLEMENTARY FOODS FOR BIRDS

	Bread/ breadcrumbs	Broken biscuits	Cake	Suet	Bacon (incl. hanging fat)	Cheese	Raisins/sultanas	Apples/pears	Potato	Kitchen scraps
Pheasant	✓									✓
Woodpigeon	✓	✓								✓
Collared dove	✓	✓	✓	✓					✓	
Great spotted woodpecker				✓	✓					
Wren	✓	✓	✓	✓		✓				
Dunnock	✓	✓	✓	✓	✓	✓		✓	✓	✓
Robin	✓	✓	✓	✓	✓	✓	✓	✓	✓	✓
Blackbird	✓	✓	✓	✓	✓	✓	✓	✓	✓	✓
Song thrush	✓	✓	✓	✓	✓	✓	✓	✓	✓	✓
Redwing	✓	✓			✓			✓		✓
Blackcap	✓			✓	✓	✓	✓	✓	✓	✓
Long-tailed tit	✓			✓	✓	✓				
Marsh tit	✓	✓		✓						
Coal tit				✓	✓	✓		✓		
Blue tit	✓	✓	✓	✓	✓	✓		✓	✓	
Great tit	✓			✓	✓	✓		✓	✓	
Nuthatch	✓	✓	✓	✓	✓			✓	✓	
Magpie	✓	✓			✓		✓	✓		✓
Jackdaw	✓	✓	✓	✓	✓	✓	✓	✓	✓	✓
Starling	✓	✓	✓	✓	✓	✓	✓	✓	✓	✓
House sparrow	✓	✓	✓	✓	✓	✓			✓	✓
Chaffinch	✓	✓	✓	✓	✓	✓		✓	✓	✓
Brambling	✓				✓					
Greenfinch	✓		✓					✓		
Goldfinch								✓		
Siskin					✓	✓				

FURTHER BIRDS RECORDED AS FEEDING ON SUPPLEMENTARY FOODS

(List includes some accidentals in Britain and only some foods)

Heron	Meat
Mute swan	Bread, cake, cheese
Greylag goose	Bread, cake, kitchen scraps
Canada goose	Bread, cake
Mallard	Bread, cake, scraps
Tufted duck	Bread, cake, scraps
Kestrel	Meat
Water rail	Bread, kitchen scraps
Moorhen	Bread, corn
American purple gallinule	Food scraps
Coot	Bread, potato
Black-headed gull	Bread, cake, potato, seed
Common gull	Bread, cake
Lesser black-backed gull	Bread
Herring gull	Bread, biscuits
Great black-backed gull	Bread
Feral pigeon	Bread, biscuit, peanut, banana, apple, chocolate, fat
Stock dove	Bread, seed
Ring-necked parakeet	Peanut, seed, apple
Tawny owl	Meat bones
Green woodpecker	Peanuts
Lesser spotted woodpecker	Peanut, sunflower seed, fat, suet
Skylark	Bread, cheese, small seed, wheat, fruit
Meadow pipit	Bread, small seed, suet
Grey wagtail	Bread, seed, fat, potato
Pied wagtail	Bread, seed, fat, potato, porridge
Waxwing	Fruit, peanuts
Fieldfare	Fruits (incl. apple, pear, raspberry)
Mistle thrush	Bread, apple
Black redstart	Meat, fat, fruit
Stonechat	Seed
Lesser whitethroat	Peanut, fat, suet
Chiffchaff	Bread, fat, scraps
Goldcrest	Peanut fragments, cheese, fat, breadcrumbs
Firecrest	Breadcrumbs, fat
Willow tit	Coconut, peanut, sunflower seed, bread, suet
Crested tit	Seed, fat, meat
Treecreeper	Peanut granules, bread, fat, suet
Jay	Bread, peanuts, potato, porridge, etc.
Rook	Bread, scraps, etc.
Carrion/hooded crow	Any food scraps
Spanish sparrow	Bread, seed, kitchen scraps
Tree sparrow	Seed, peanuts, bread, fat
Serin	Seed
Linnet	Small seed
Redpoll	Small seed
Bullfinch	Breadcrumbs, ripe fruit
Hawfinch	Peanuts, large seeds, dried fruit
Dark-eyed junco	Seed
Yellowhammer	Seed, corn, dried fruit
Cirl bunting	Seed
Reed bunting	Bread, cake, pastry, seed
Corn bunting	Dried fruit, seed, corn

FURTHER SUPPLEMENTARY FOODS FOR BIRDS

Cornflakes	Jackdaw
Rice krispies	Robin, jackdaw
Weetabix/fat mixture	Grey wagtail
Macaroni cheese	Blackbird
Porridge	Treecreeper, jackdaw, house sparrow
Parsnip soup	Song thrush
Ants' eggs	Green woodpecker
Dog cereal food, puppy meal	Popular generally
Pastry	Treecreeper and others
Oranges	Fieldfare
Cooked rice, no salt	Various
Ice cream	Feral pigeon and gulls
Acorns	Jay
Teasel seeds	Goldfinch

SUPPLEMENTARY AIDS TO NESTING AND ROOSTING

Birds benefit from extra roosting and nesting sites in a garden. Additional places for shelter and a range of different types of nest boxes are invaluable to birds, as most gardens are short on these commodities. Even so, it is extremely unlikely that every site provided will be used. Usage depends on many different factors: the location of the nest site (which must be within a bird's territory), the size, the situation of the entrance to the nest, the temperature (which must be neither too hot nor too cold), the amount of cover provided and the available perches. A lot of factors depend on the species and even on the individuals!

Nest boxes

Many birds that regularly visit our gardens are woodland birds, which naturally nest in crevices and holes in trees. In the garden, artificial, ready-made nest boxes provide safe alternative nest sites for many of these species; the blue tit is the most frequent user. Other birds will also use nest boxes, subject to their shape, size and position, which must suit their requirements.

Small, open-fronted boxes may attract pied wagtails, robins, spotted flycatchers and wrens whilst small boxes, with an entrance hole of less than $1\frac{1}{8}$in (28mm) in diameter, may be used by blue, coal, marsh or willow tit. Boxes with larger

A nest box suitable for robins.

The diameter of the circular hole varies to attract different birds.

entrance holes, not exceeding 1³⁄₁₆ in (30mm)
in diameter, may persuade the great tit or the
increasingly scarce tree sparrow to nest if
they are placed in the right environs.

(Above) Blue tits will readily accept the
shelter of a nesting box and can occupy
the same location year after year.

(Right) Robins like to nest in overhanging
vegetation so their nest boxes should be
well covered and camouflaged.

Larger boxes may be occupied by house sparrow, nuthatch, pied flycatcher and redstart to name just a few. It is even possible to have boxes made for woodpecker and ringed-neck parakeet.

All manner of differently shaped and sized nest boxes are available (or can be constructed) – from the large kestrel platforms and barn owl boxes that must be positioned at least 16ft (5m) above the ground, to the unusual tube-shaped tawny owl box. The artificial swallow and house martin nests, shaped like a half cup, can be attached under the eaves of buldings. Take care when purchasing these more unusual boxes: dippers may take up residence in a dipper box, but only if it is in the right environment, otherwise there will be no dippers about. We have had two artificial house martin nests up beneath the eaves for years and not once have they been occupied. There was a large colony of birds over the road but they chose not to come to us. That house martin colony diminished and finally disappeared. Our plastic nests are now often used by blue tits as a place to shelter during storms. We have watched them fly up and disappear inside at the onset of heavy rain or snow.

BIRDWATCHER'S TIP

|||||||||||||||||||||||||||||||||||||||||||||||||||||||||||||||||||||||||||||||||||||||||||

Great spotted woodpeckers are capable of creating holes in wooden boxes to steal the fledglings within. If woodpeckers are a menace, it may be advisable to purchase a box made from woodcrete – a mixture of concrete and sawdust. These boxes, though not so pleasing to the eye, are waterproof, long-lasting and impenetrable to such attack.

(Above) A large nest box in a rural location being visited by one of the birds busy collecting material to build a nest inside.

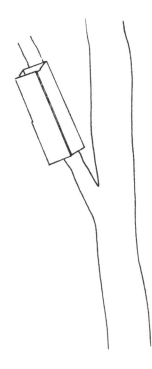

(Above) Tawny owls naturally make their nests in a deep, dark tree cavity. The nest box for a tawny owl should be situated high up on a trunk or major branch in or near woodland.

(Right) A nest box made from woodcrete is designed for attaching to a tree trunk or suspending from a branch. Woodcrete keeps the nest box safe from woodpeckers.

If there are swifts in your neighbourhood, they may be encouraged to take up residence in a swift box positioned under the eaves of a tall building. This elongate rectangular box has a narrow entrance slit of no more than 1³/₁₆in (30mm) in height at one end. As swifts return from their spring migration slightly later than other birds (during late April and early May) they may find that house sparrows, like squatters, have already taken up residence in the box. To prevent this, erect the box a week before their expected return.

Most nest boxes are made from wood at least ⁵/₈in (15mm) thick. This gives some insulation and prevents the wood warping in damp conditions.

Making a basic nest box

A basic nest box can be constructed using a plank of wood roughly 51¼ x 5⅞ x ⅝in (1,300 x 150 x 15mm). Cut the wood so that the grain runs vertically down the sides of the box. This helps the water run off and thus keeps it from seeping into the wood. Blue tits will need an entrance hole between 1 and 1⅛in (25 and 28mm) in diameter, with the top of the hole 1³⁄₁₆–1½in (30–40mm) below the lid. If the hole is any larger, bigger birds, like the house sparrow and great tit, may oust the smaller birds. (For the nest box requirements of different bird species see table on page 123.)

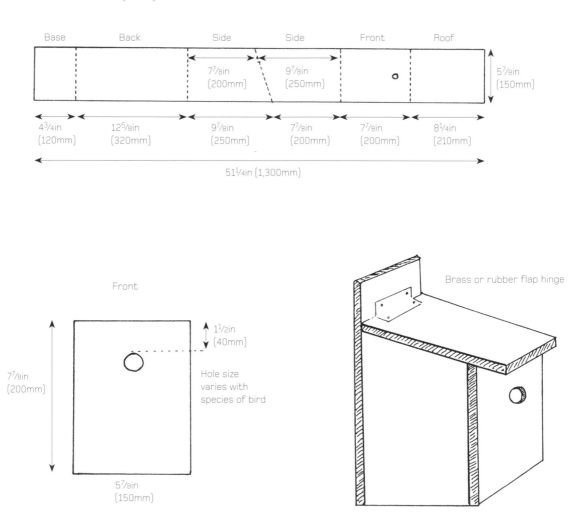

Width of wood: ⅝in (15mm)

| Base | Back | Side | Side | Front | Roof |

7⅞in (200mm)   9⅞in (250mm)

5⅞in (150mm)

4¾in (120mm)   12⅝in (320mm)   9⅞in (250mm)   7⅞in (200mm)   7⅞in (200mm)   8¼in (210mm)

51¼in (1,300mm)

Front

1½in (40mm)

Hole size varies with species of bird

7⅞in (200mm)

5⅞in (150mm)

Brass or rubber flap hinge

A basic, small nest box

Making an open-fronted nest box

The construction of robin and spotted flycatcher boxes is similar to that of the basic nest box except at the front where a piece of wood (4 x 5⅞in [100 x 150mm] for robins and 2 x 5⅞in [50 x 150mm] for spotted flycatchers) is fixed to the lower half to make an open-fronted box.

These boxes need to be placed in quiet, secluded spots, perhaps on walls, half hidden by the foliage of climbing shrubs. Spotted flycatchers are shy summer migrants of deciduous woodland and gardens but they have drastically reduced in number over the past 25 years, and have vanished from many areas where they used to breed.

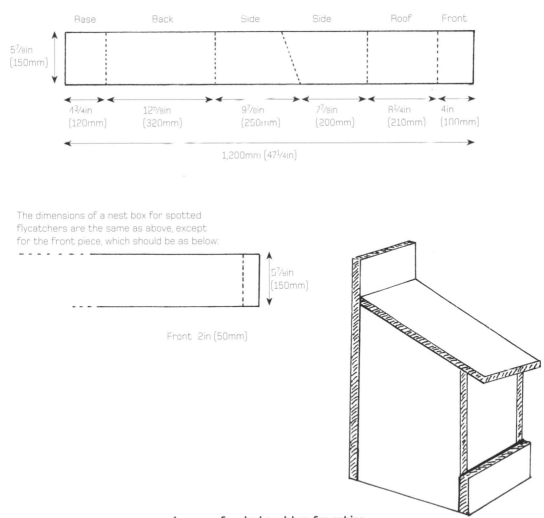

Width of wood: ⅝in (15mm)

Base   Back   Side   Side   Roof   Front

5⅞in (150mm)

1¾in (120mm)   12⅝in (320mm)   9⅞in (250mm)   7⅞in (200mm)   8¼in (210mm)   4in (100mm)

1,200mm (47¼in)

The dimensions of a nest box for spotted flycatchers are the same as above, except for the front piece, which should be as below:

5⅞in (150mm)

Front 2in (50mm)

An open-fronted nest box for robins

REQUIREMENTS FOR NEST BOX CONSTRUCTION AND MAINTENANCE

- Two or more drainage holes are needed in the bottom of the box for ventilation and for draining away moisture.

- A sloping, overhanging roof is needed to prevent drips of rain running down inside.

- The box must have some method of opening so that it can be cleaned. Annual maintenance is important, as old nests harbour parasites that can infect next year's chicks. Remove the old nest in autumn and, if necessary, clean the box with boiling water. Never use insecticides: even small amounts of insecticide are potentially harmful to chicks in the nest.

- Place a small amount of grass or wood shavings in the bottom of the box. This will help with insulation and make it a more appealing roosting site for birds over winter.

- To make the box last longer, the outside of it can be treated with wood preservative, but never treat the insides: it is not known what effect preservatives have on birds, but it can kill bats.

- Do not put two nest boxes of the same type next to each other, as birds become territorial during the nesting season. The best position for a box is a quieter part of the garden away as much as possible from human disturbance. Position the box so that the entrance does not face the prevailing wind and is not directly facing the midday sun. This may cause the poor fledglings to roast and suffocate in the height of summer!

- Try to disguise the box by growing climbers around it. Honeysuckle, clematis and ivy are good examples. These will provide the box with extra seclusion, hiding it away from the roving eyes of predators.

OTHER ARTIFICIAL NEST SITES

Some birds are very adaptable and will nest wherever there is an opportunity. Robins will often nest in the most peculiar places: a discarded old boot, an abandoned watering can, an old kettle out of sight in the midst of a thicket. One year a pair of robins successfully raised a brood amongst the stacked pots in our greenhouse. Last year a blackbird was successful nesting against the wall on the lawn mower in a neighbour's garage. I have seen blue tits nest in street lamps and under the roofing felt on a flat roof. Birds are great opportunists.

TYPES OF NEST BOX

	Entrance hole	Open-fronted	Size: large (L), medium (M) or small (S)	
Kestrel		✓	L	Place 17ft+ (5m+) above ground on wall or tree
Ring-necked parakeet	✓		L	Hole size $3\frac{1}{8}$in (80mm)
Tawny owl		✓	L	Place tube-shaped box in mature tree
Pied wagtail		✓	S	Needs open position overlooking lawn
Wren		✓	S	Will roost in tit boxes
Robin		✓	S	Needs a secluded position hidden by climbers or shrubbery
Spotted flycatcher		✓	S	Needs climber-covered wall overlooking lawn
Pied flycatcher	✓		S/M	Hole size $1\frac{1}{8}$–$1\frac{3}{16}$in (28–30mm)
Marsh tit	✓		S	Hole size 1–$1\frac{1}{8}$in (25–28mm)
Willow tit	✓		S	Hole size 1–$1\frac{1}{8}$in (25–28mm): infill box with wood shavings
Coal tit	✓			Hole size 1–$1\frac{1}{8}$in (25–28mm)
Blue tit	✓		S	Hole size 1–$1\frac{1}{8}$in (25–28mm)
Great tit	✓		S	Hole size $1\frac{1}{8}$–$1\frac{3}{16}$in (28–30mm)
Nuthatch	✓		M	Hole size $1\frac{1}{4}$in+ (32mm+)
Treecreeper	✓		M	Triangular-shaped box with side hole
Starling	✓		M	Hole size $1\frac{3}{4}$in (45mm)
House sparrow	✓		M	Hole size $1\frac{1}{4}$in (32mm)
Tree sparrow	✓		S	Hole size $1\frac{1}{8}$–$1\frac{3}{16}$in (28–30mm)

PONDS AND BOG GARDENS

Water is a basic necessity in a birdwatcher's garden: all birds need water to drink and bathe. Large water features and ponds may attract a greater variety of birds and other wildlife, creating a distinct habitat. In secluded gardens with a stream or damp ditch, moorhen, mallard and even snipe may come to visit. River, canal and lakeside gardens may have mute swan, duck, greylag and Canada geese snoozing or grazing on the lawns and reed bunting and warblers singing from nearby bushes. Kingfisher may pass up and down river in a dart of dazzling blue. There may be little grebe skulking under shrubs at the water's edge, grey wagtail flitting from one bank to the next, or a heron standing motionless on the riverbank, concentrating on fishing.

Migrating birds often follow water courses during their spring and autumn journeys. Great numbers of hirundines (including swallow, house martin and sand martin) and waders (greenshank, redshank, lapwing, oystercatcher and sandpipers) may be seen on passage. One spring we watched an osprey flying low over our garden, being mobbed by two loudly shrieking herring gulls. This osprey was flying down river on the return journey to its breeding ground in Scotland. It was an incredible sight and proves that there can be an element of surprise in birdwatching. Always look out for the unexpected.

For those who are not so fortunate as to have waterside gardens, creating a wildlife pond may be the most suitable alternative. Generally, where space allows, the bigger the pond the easier it is to maintain. Care should be taken with young children and toddlers as any pool of water can be extremely hazardous. If there are young children about, it is advisable to postpone pond building for a few years and, in the meantime, provide a shallow birdbath instead.

(Opposite, top) The reed bunting is typically found near wet ground. When singing, the male perches on top of a reed or bush.

(Opposite) Creating a pond is becoming an increasingly important way to make a haven for wildlife.

Swift

Swallow

House martin

Sand martin

European birds fly south to spend the winter in warm climates. Migrating birds can cover several hundred miles per day in flight.

Destruction of natural water sites

Creating a pond in the garden is becoming increasingly important, as many natural water features have been lost in the open countryside. It has been estimated by English Nature (Natural England) that about 75 per cent of areas of standing water of less than 2½ acres (one hectare) has been lost during the last 100 years. Ponds have been filled in, ploughed up and drained for agriculture and for industrial and housing developments; while many more have been neglected and have silted up or become otherwise polluted. This has destroyed the natural balance of wildlife irreversibly.

Pollution is often caused by agricultural chemicals (fertilizers, fungicides, herbicides and pesticides) used on neighbouring fields seeping into the water and causing contamination, and by run-off from silage. Silage is a winter green fodder (grass, lucerne, maize, etc.) stored in airtight

Natural water features, such as this duck pond, are vanishing from the countryside.

conditions in a clamp or silo. 'Silage liquor' is high in nitrogen and has extremely corrosive properties. If any leakage occurs it can cause severe organic pollution to ponds and water courses. Many of our, once common, 400 species of associated higher plants and six amphibians (frog, common and natterjack toads, great crested, palmate and smooth newts), and as many as 2,000 species of invertebrate (including dragonflies, damselflies, water boatmen, water beetles and water snails) are becoming increasingly scarce in rural areas as ponds vanish. The ever-rising demand for water by both industrial and domestic users has led to an increase in its extraction. Coupled with the recent years of drought, which have not helped, this has been detrimental to many small wetland sites.

Birds are very much part of this habitat. Coot and moorhen will vanish once their food plants are unavailable. Swallow and house martin may be unable to find mud to build their nests. Herons will no longer be seen 'frogging' in long grass if the amphibian population dies out with the loss of breeding ponds as is happening, especially in the south-eastern counties of Britain.

Moorhens are ground-living birds that can be seen anywhere there is an expanse of water.

BIRDWATCHER'S TIP

All wildlife suffers when there is no available water. It is important, therefore, to create a pond in the garden, not only for the birds but also for the mammals, invertebrates and amphibians that need this sanctuary to thrive in a new garden environment.

Types of pond

Raised and formal ponds, with their steep walls, are particularly unsuitable for birds: in summer, when the water level drops, they and other creatures may not be able to reach the water in order to drink. We have watched an acrobatic blue tit stretch 3in (70mm) vertically downwards to drink from a pond edged with stones. This is impressive for a bird no more than 4^{1}/$_{2}$in (115mm) from beak to tail. Not all birds are this agile. Many spend much time hopping around the pond, unable to reach the water.

Moulded fibreglass ponds, more expensive than flexible liners, are readily available in most garden centres in various shapes and sizes. For the same reason, these too may be unsuitable. The steeply sloping sides prevent easy access for birds wishing to bathe and drink, and without one gently sloping side, a pond will be hazardous for other creatures: if they accidentally fall in, they will be unable to clamber out and consequently will drown. Hedgehogs, it seems, are particularly prone to blunder into ponds. However, this problem can be rectified by building up a gentle slope of stones and pebbles on one side to provide creatures with access into and out of the water.

The best type of pond for birds and other wildlife is one made from a flexible liner so that the shape can be adapted to suit particular requirements. Flexible liners are available in butyl (long-lasting), PVC and polythene. Polythene liners are the cheapest but they may only last for a couple of years.

Mini ponds

Mini ponds are also worth considering where space is at a premium. Small ponds can be made by sinking any watertight container into the ground; anything from a dustbin lid or half a barrel to an old sink. Add a few aquatic plants to create a mini habitat for many creatures – even a frog may take up residence. No matter how small the pond, it must have one gently sloping edge to enable birds, mammals and amphibians to get into and out of the water.

In our garden we have a mini, 'L' shaped, ditch-like pond made from the remnants of the flexible liner we used for our larger pond. This mini pond is less than 12in (300mm) deep, has a narrow, sloping beach of pebbles (small stones gathered from the garden), and is planted up with a few oxygenators – starwort (*Callitriche* spp.), crowfoot (*Ranunculus aquatilis*) and a bit

Water starwort (*Callitriche* sp.)

(Right) A dustbin lid set into the grass becomes an ideal bathing and drinking area for birds.

of goldfish weed (*Lagarosiphon major*). There are also two smaller marginal plants: water plantain (*Alisma plantago-aquatica*) and brooklime (*Veronica beccabunga*). With a pond this size it is easy to keep most plants under control, although we did make one mistake: we added a little fairy moss (*Azolla filiculoides*) which exploded into growth during the warm summer months, covering the water surface. We had to remove this every four or five days. All sorts of birds are attracted to our mini pond, from crows to thrushes and tits. A male bullfinch has even come down to the water's edge once or twice.

Our bog garden, in a sunken plastic baby bath (with the plug left in), is planted with brooklime, marsh marigold (*Caltha palustris*) and monkey flower (*Mimulus guttatus*), all of which thrive.

Dustbin lids dug into the lawn or border also make excellent mini ponds and birdbaths. Be sure to place some stones in the bottom so that the smaller birds, and even butterflies, may perch on the edge to absorb some moisture. We put a tiny amount of goldfish weed in the water to help keep it clear. Keep the water topped up, as it evaporates quickly during summer. Even a pool this size will contain an abundance of aquatic life: water snails, midge larvae, drone fly larvae and the rat-tailed maggot (*Eristalis* sp.) characterized by its plump white body and long, rat-like tail which protrudes to the water surface. We experienced a puzzling mystery with our mini pond. Every morning we would find piles of goldfish weed drying out on the grass.

The mystery remained unsolved until, eventually, we caught the culprit at work. A crow was carefully removing all the pieces of weed from the water before feasting on those rat-tailed maggots!

Birdbaths

The importance of providing water for birds throughout the year cannot be over-estimated. If there is no room for a pond in your garden, any type of container can be used to hold water, from saucers, old kitchen bowls and frying pans to purpose-built birdbaths, whether they be cheap and practical items or highly ornate statuary. Ensure that the container is secure and will not topple when any large bird lands. With larger containers, place one flat stone or a few pebbles in the bottom to provide different depths of water for birds to bathe. Any containers used should be washed out regularly and refilled with clean water to prevent the spread of disease.

Care and siting of ponds

Site the pond in an open, sunny position, away from most overhanging trees and shrubs, to reduce the problem of leaves in the autumn. Many pond plants grow weak and spindly in shady conditions and may not flower. However, it is important to provide some cover near the water's edge to enable the more timid birds to come.

(Top right) A bird bath is used by garden birds to dip their wings and splash water on their backs.

(Right) Brooklime (*Veronica beccabunga*)

Leaves and rotting vegetation are problematic in autumn and winter. Even ponds in open spaces can collect leaves that rot to form a nasty sludge in the bottom. Rotting vegetation removes oxygen from the water and, as it breaks down, releases nutrients that encourage algal growth. In extreme cases ponds become eutrophic, developing into dark, noxious, pungent pools, smelling of bad eggs (due to the hydrogen sulphide and sulphur dioxide they release) and bubbling from the bottom with marsh gas (methane). Sometimes these bubbles ignite – these pale flames are known as will-o'-the-wisp

Due to the lack of oxygen in such water, little aquatic life can survive and the pond becomes less attractive to birds, and humans too! Before a pond comes anywhere near this state, it should be drained and cleared during the autumn. Take care to leave some mud on the bottom, as there might be a frog hibernating in the pond bed. It may be necessary to half drain a pond to remove all the rotted matter, but again, be careful not to disturb the bottom too much. This retrieved decomposed matter should be left on the edge of the pond for a few hours so that the numerous wiggly aquatic creatures can scamper back in.

Autumn is also the time to cut back and remove all the dying vegetation, water lily leaves and other pond plant foliage so that it does not decompose in the water. Aquatic plants can be restocked in April or May.

The practice of covering ponds with a fine mesh netting in autumn and winter may solve the problem of rotting leaves, but it denies birds access to the water. Netting is also dangerous for many unsuspecting animals. Birds, hedgehogs, grass snakes in southern England and even eels on their migration may become trapped and fatally entangled. It is therefore advisable not to cover ponds with netting but to remove leaves regularly during autumn with the aid of a small net.

Marsh marigold (*Caltha palustris*) is found near water.

Pond layout

If garden ponds are to provide a useful and safe water source for wildlife and birds they must meet a number of requirements. (See illustration below.) They must have:

• a gently sloping shallow edge;
• shelves for marginal plants;
• deep water;
• a bog garden close by.

Gently sloping shallow edge

A shallow slope is necessary to provide birds and mammals an area of access to the pond for drinking and bathing. A gentle slope will also enable frogs, toads, newts and mammals, like the hedgehog, that accidentally blunder in, to get back out of the water.

Shelves for marginal plants

Shelves of 4–12in (100–300mm) deep around the pond will provide an environment for flowering marginal plants to grow. Where the depth of water is about 4in (100mm), plants can be planted directly into the pond soil. A deeper shelf is needed for those aquatic marginals that have been planted up in plastic mesh baskets so that the containers do not show above the water level. These will attract a wide assortment of insects and the seed heads provide food for birds. Damselfly and dragonfly nymphs clamber up the stems of iris, rush or reed on emerging from the water, to metamorphose into adults. Shelves will also provide a spawning area for frogs and water beetles. Tadpoles provide food for all manner of ducks, herons and thrushes as well as many aquatic creatures, such as dragonfly nymphs, great diving beetles, newts, fish and water shrews.

Deep water

A pond should include a section where the water is at least 18–30in (450–750mm) deep. This will ensure that the pond does not freeze solid during winter, enabling newts and male frogs to

Layout for a garden pond

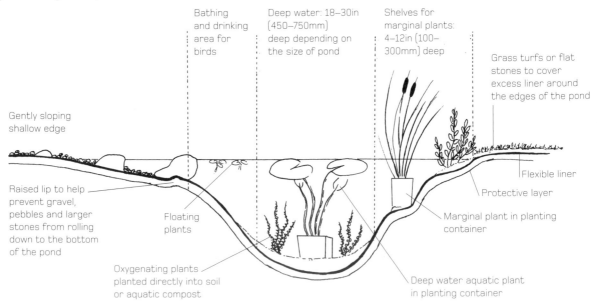

Bathing and drinking area for birds

Deep water: 18–30in (450–750mm) deep depending on the size of pond

Shelves for marginal plants: 4–12in (100–300mm) deep

Grass turfs or flat stones to cover excess liner around the edges of the pond

Gently sloping shallow edge

Raised lip to help prevent gravel, pebbles and larger stones from rolling down to the bottom of the pond

Floating plants

Oxygenating plants planted directly into soil or aquatic compost

Flexible liner

Protective layer

Marginal plant in planting container

Deep water aquatic plant in planting container

hibernate in the muddy bottom. If ice covers the pond for long periods the oxygen levels in the water will be depleted and these amphibians may suffocate, their dead bodies found floating on the water surface once the thaw comes. To prevent this, always ensure that there is a patch of clear water so that the noxious gases that accumulate under the ice can escape. Never break the ice with a hammer or stone: the shock waves from the ice shattering can be harmful to fish and the other aquatic creatures in the water. Instead, place a pan full of hot water on the ice to create a hole. Clear any ice from around the edge of the pond so the birds have some access to the water. In winter, with snow about, accessible water may be very limited. In such conditions, birds that are not usually associated with gardens may descend in search of fresh water. One dark, cold winter's morning in our garden, a whole flock of siskins arrived and descended to drink from the pond for a few moments before flying off once more. They ignored the plentiful supply of peanuts and all the other foodstuffs.

Bog gardens

A bog garden will aid wildlife and make the pond as natural as possible by providing an area of damp, marshy ground or bog next to the water. This makes the whole area more attractive to amphibians, especially if a pile of logs or stones is placed nearby so they can rest through the day in the moist shade and have a place for hibernation during winter. Mud from the garden may be collected by swallows and house martins for nest building and by the blackbird to line her nest. The type of plants you wish to grow will affect the level of dampness you require. Some plants will not survive waterlogging. For these plants, therefore, the soil must be kept damp but should never be allowed to become truly waterlogged. Other plants will survive waterlogging and thus

can be grown in a more boggy garden. A 'drier' bog garden is made using a pond liner, which should be perforated with a few drainage holes and filled with a water-retentive soil. Suitable wildflower plants for this area include bistort (*Persicaria bistorta, syn. Polygonum bistorta*), creeping Jenny (*Lysimachia nummularia*), cuckoo flower (*Cardamine pratensis*), hemp agrimony (*Eupatorium cannabinum*), meadow-sweet (*Filipendula ulmaria*), purple loosestrife (*Lythrum salicaria*) and ragged robin (*Lychnis flos-cuculi*). (See the table on page 136.) Other garden plants to grow in these conditions include *Astilbe*, *Iris sibirica*, hosta, mimulus and primula. It may be necessary to keep watering the area during summer to keep the soil from drying out.

It is advisable to use two pieces of pond liner for a pond and for this type of bog garden so as to keep the water level from continually dropping.

The damper alternative should be made using an unperforated liner. Only plants that can survive some waterlogging should be grown in this type of garden. Such plants include many marginal plants as shown in the table on page 137.

Ragged robin
(Lychnis flos-cuculi)

CONSTRUCTING A POND WITH A FLEXIBLE LINER

1 Mark out the shape of the pond with a hose pipe, or pegs and string, on level ground away from overhanging trees. Dig out the pond to shape, slightly deeper than required to compensate for the protective layer and liner.

2 Ensure that all the top edges of the pond are level, using a plank of wood and a spirit level.

3 Remove any sharp stones and protruding roots from the sides of the pond, as these may pierce and ruin the liner.

4 Lay a protective covering of thick newspaper, old carpet and sieved soil or sand around the sides and on the bottom before spreading the flexible liner on top.

The length of liner needed for a simple-shaped pond can be calculated by measuring the greatest length and adding on twice the greatest depth plus at least 24in (600mm). This will give a margin of 12in (300mm) around the edge, which will allow for the folds in the liner and prevent leakage. Likewise, the width of liner required can be calculated by measuring the greatest width and adding on twice the greatest depth plus 24in (600mm) for the margin.

Liner length = greatest pond length + (depth x 2) + 24in (600mm)

Liner width = greatest pond width + (depth x 2) + 24in (600mm)

When the liner is laid, cut away any excess.

5 Cover the bottom of the pond with a thin layer of aquatic compost or subsoil to allow the plants to root and spread naturally. The shallow edge may be covered with grit and small pebbles to make it look more attractive, though we have found that with the force of blackbirds' frequent ablutions, stones and grit soon tumble down the gentle gradient, exposing the unsightly liner. A 'beach' of larger stones in this region of shallow water will help the smaller birds reach the water's edge.

6 Fill the pond with rain water, either naturally with falling rain or with water collected from a water butt. When natural deluges of rain are not forthcoming, tap water is often used for filling ponds. However, tap water contains harmful chemicals, so the pond should be left a couple of weeks for these to degenerate before any plants can be introduced.

Pond flora

A healthy, balanced pond needs plants. Native plants will attract a greater diversity of wildlife, providing food from shoots, leaves, buds and seeds. In warm weather conditions algae thrive. When allowed to grow unchecked, algae will turn many ponds into a harmful and unsightly, thick, green, pea soup. Algae in this state will deprive many aquatic creatures of necessary oxygen, which will have a knock-on effect up the food chain, reaching birds and other mammals. Appropriate planting will reduce the problem of algal blooms.

Oxygenating plants

These plants will aerate the water and, through competition, will help starve algae of the carbon dioxide and minerals that they need to flourish. Oxygenating plants include water hornwort (*Ceratophyllum demersum*), water crowfoot (*Ranunculus aquatilis*), pondweed (*Potamogeton* spp.), water milfoil (*Myriophyllum spicatum*) and water starwort (*Callitriche* spp.). Canadian pondweed (*Elodea canadensis*) and goldfish weed (*Lagarosiphon major*) are not native but both are good oxygenating plants. (See table on page 136.)

Goldfish weed (*Lagarosiphon major*)

Deep-water aquatics

Water lilies and plants of lily-like habit will help by creating shade, which discourages algal growth. The water lily (*Nymphaea alba*), fringed water lily/ villarsia (*Nymphoides peltata*) and water violet (*Hottonia palustris*) are all examples of deep-water aquatics native to Britain.

Floating plants

Floating plants may have the same effect, depriving the algae of light and thus discouraging growth. In nutrient-rich conditions some of these plants are liable to grow rampantly, covering the water surface completely in no time. Duckweeds, great (*Lemna polyrrhiza*) and lesser (*L. minor*), should perhaps be avoided, with the exception of ivy-leaved duckweed (*L. trisulca*). They are, however, a plant food for coot, moorhen, mallard, greylag goose and water rail. Even fairy moss (*Azolla filiculoides*), the water fern introduced from the United States, can explode into growth in warm weather. This fern is not particularly hardy; it may be advisable to keep a small amount in a water-tight container, in frost-free conditions, over the cold winter months. Other floating plants with less invasive habits include frogbit (*Hydrocharis morsus-ranae*) and water soldier (*Stratiotes aloides*).

Marginal plants

Around the pond's edges, plants are needed for cover and as food to attract birds and insects. Suitable marginal plants include bur reeds (*Sparganium* spp.), club-rushes (*Scirpus* spp.), reeds (*Phragmites* spp.), bulrush/reedmace (*Typha* spp.), rushes (*Juncus* spp.) and sedges (*Carex* spp.). The seeds of all these plants can provide food for sparrows, finches and reed bunting as well as other water birds. Many of these plants may be too vigorous for consideration in a small garden pond but there are less rampant alternatives such as the corkscrew rush (*Juncus spiralis*) and dwarf reedmace (*Typha minima*). Bur reeds have strong, sharp-growing shoots and strong rhizomes that are capable of growing through plastic planting containers and puncturing the flexible liner, so you may wish to avoid these plants.

When buying aquatic plants, always check the ultimate size and spread. Flowering marginals to consider include arrowhead (*Sagittaria sagittifolia*), brooklime (*Veronica beccabunga*), flowering rush (*Butomus umbellatus*), marsh marigold/kingcup (*Caltha palustris*), water forget-me-not (*Myosotis scorpioides*), water mint (*Mentha aquatica*), water plantain (*Alisma plantago-aquatica*) and yellow flag iris (*Iris pseudacorus*). (See the table on page 137.) *Iris laevigata*, not a native to Britain, grows well and should not be neglected. Many marginal pond plants will survive out of the water in a bog garden, providing the soil is kept moist.

In smaller ponds, deep-water aquatics and marginal plants may be planted up in special containers that will help inhibit their spread. Make sure you use soil or aquatic compost for planting. Never use nutrient-rich potting composts, as this will encourage the growth of algae, duckweeds and blanket weeds.

Bur reeds *(Sparganium)* grow in still or slow-flowing water.

A well-established pond may naturally attract pond creatures such as frogs and toads.

Pond fauna

Stocking fish will have a detrimental effect on birds and other wildlife. Fish eat tadpoles and plenty of insect larvae, and thus deprive birds of food. Conversely, a passing heron may delight in removing all the goldfish or koi from a pond for its supper. Even kingfishers have been known to raid ponds, and thus the pond becomes a very expensive bird table!

Introducing pond snail ramshorns (*Planorbis* sp.) and pond snails (*Limnaea* sp.) is beneficial, as they help control algal growth, though they also nibble at certain pond plants like the water lily and frogbit. Blackbirds and other thrushes will eat these snails.

Other pond creatures, including frogs, toads and newts, damselflies and dragonflies, may find their way to the pond if they are in the vicinity. Smaller aquatic creatures may be introduced when the pond plants are added. Another way of creating a diverse community is to add a bucketful of mud and water from a neighbour's established garden pond.

Bird activity

Feeding habits

A few birds need water to moisten their food and to make it easier to swallow. We watched a carrion crow dunking dried cubes of bread in a shallow birdbath before devouring them and setting off to a neighbouring garden for more. This left a mass of soggy breadcrumbs floating in the water, but immediately the crow had left, an opportunist female blackbird arrived to quickly gulp up the crumbs.

Bathing habits

There are some birds that will bathe and splash about in the water whatever the weather conditions. We have watched blue and great tits, blackbirds, song thrushes, chaffinches and greenfinches taking the plunge even in heavy rain. In icy winter weather (when the water wasn't completely frozen) a female blackbird enjoyed her daily splash in conditions we would certainly think twice about!

House sparrows are gregarious creatures and seem to enjoy splashing about in the water together for some time. Some birds emerge so wet and bedraggled that they need to spend much time thereafter drying out in the sunshine on the top of the hedge, preening to keep their feathers in trim. Dunnocks routinely take ablutions as do blue tits, either from the shallows or by lowering themselves into the pond water whilst clinging to a stalk of a marginal plant.

The nuthatch is a more secretive bird and will only bathe in the most secluded corner of our garden pond. A quick dip into the water, a flap of the wings and it is out and back to the safety of the shrubbery. This process is repeated once or twice, but each time the bird is cautious.

One of the most regular bathers in our garden is the blackbird. Each morning our local population of blackbirds seems to take it in turns to have a dip, with the most dominant bird chasing any other blackbird or passing song thrush away from the vicinity until the bathing is complete. Blackbirds venture slightly deeper into the water than the smaller garden birds, and their vigorous flapping and splashing sprays water over a much greater distance. Other birds seem not to mind this. We have observed a female chaffinch and a house sparrow perch nearby on a stone, receiving the full benefit of an effort-free shower!

The action of bathing and the subsequent preening and oiling of feathers helps to maintain the bird's condition and keeps the number of feather mites, fleas, lice and mites (the ecto-parasites) in check. A highly parasitized bird has less chance of survival than a healthy one.

THE BENEFITS OF SUNSHINE

On warm, sunny days some species of bird like to sunbathe. Collared doves, sparrows, finches and thrushes may be seen lying prostrate on the grass or border, limp and motionless, their bills open and with slightly outstretched wings. Just like humans, these birds enjoy the sunshine and it does have some health benefits for them. It has been suggested that the warmth of the sun makes birds' parasites more active and thus easier to remove with preening.

PLANTS THAT THRIVE IN MOIST BUT NOT SATURATED SOILS

PLANT	FLOWERING TIME	DESCRIPTION
Bistort (*Persicaria bistorta*)	June–October	Perennial, spikes of tiny pink flowers. A plant food of collared dove, crow, finches, sparrows, pheasant, partridge, coot and moorhen.
Creeping Jenny (*Lysimachia nummularia*)	June–August	Low-growing, creeping perennial with yellow flowers. Good for growing over stones around the edge of ponds.
Cuckoo flower (*Cardamine pratensis*)	April–June	Also known as lady's smock. Pretty, pink-flowering perennial. A food plant for the green-veined white and orange tip butterflies.
Hemp agrimony (*Eupatorium cannabinum*)	July–September	Tall, pink-flowering perennial, attractive to insects and butterflies.
Meadowsweet (*Filipendula ulmaria*)	July–September	Tall, creamy-flowering perennial. A food plant for many finches and reed bunting.
Purple loosestrife (*Lythrum salicaria*)	June–August	Perennial. Tall spikes of purple flowers and seeds for linnet and twite.
Ragged robin (*Lychnis flos-cuculi*)	May–August	Delicate, pink-flowering perennial. Good on damp, grassy areas.

OXYGENATING PLANTS

Pondweed (*Potamogeton spp.*)	Submerged, larger-leaved perennials. Plant food for geese, mallard, coot and moorhen and maybe jackdaw and carrion crow.
Water hornwort (*Ceratophyllum demersum*)	Floating, feathery-leaved rootless perennial. Plant food for coot and moorhen.
Water crowfoot (*Ranunculus aquatilis*)	Submerged feathery foliage and broader floating leaves. Yellow and white buttercup flowers from April to September. Plant food for coot and mallard.
Water milfoil (*Myriophyllum spp.*)	Submerged, feathery-leaved perennials. Plant food for coot and tufted duck.
Water starwort (*Callitriche spp.*)	Attractive, star-shaped whorls of tiny green leaves.
Canadian pondweed (*Elodea canadensis*)	Standard oxygenating plant but can be invasive. Not native. Plant food for coot.
Goldfish weed (*Lagarosiphon major*)	Similar to Canadian pondweed. Can be invasive. Plants will deteriorate with age.

FLOWERING MARGINAL PLANTS FOR POND EDGES AND BOG GARDENS

PLANTS	FLOWERING TIME	SUITABLE FOR BOG GARDENS	DESCRIPTION
Arrowhead (*Sagittaria sagittifolia*)	July–August		White-flowering perennial with arrow-shaped leaves. Plant food for mallard.
Brooklime (*Veronica beccabunga*)	May–September	✓	Creeping, blue-flowering perennial. Plant food for moorhen.
Flowering rush (*Butomus umbellatus*)	July–August		Pink-flowering perennial with rush-like leaves. Plant food for mallard.
Marsh marigold (*Caltha palustris*)	March–August	✓	Perennial with shiny yellow, buttercup flowers.
Water forget-me-not (*Myosotis scorpioides*)	June–September	✓	Perennial with pale blue flowers.
Water mint (*Mentha aquatica*)	July–September	✓	Aromatic perennial, with pink flowers. Attractive to insects.
Water plantain (*Alisma plantago-aquatica*)	June–September	✓	Perennial with pale pink flowers. Plant food for mallard and reed bunting.
Yellow flag iris (*Iris pseudacorus*)	June–August	✓	Tall, yellow-flowering perennial.

Water mint (*Mentha aquatica*)

Conserving and improving habitats is the key to preserving our wildlife. Here, the use of chemicals, peat and other potential garden hazards for birds are considered, as well the encouragement of insects beneficial to birds through the creation of wildflower meadows.

Conservation

ENVIRONMENTAL CONCERNS

In Britain since the last war, farming has become increasingly intensive and mechanized to the detriment of our native countryside. Decades of habitat destruction, with the reclamation of moorland and heathland, the drainage of wetlands, marshes and water meadows, the uprooting of hedgerows and the ploughing up of native, flower-rich meadows in favour of the monoculture of rye grass, have culminated in a great loss of wildlife.

Herbicides and pesticides

The introduction of pesticides, especially DDT during the 1950s and 1960s, has compounded this wildlife decline. Research by the then Nature Conservancy revealed a direct connection between the collapse of the peregrine population and DDT. DDT caused a thinning of the peregrine eggshells which, in turn, dramatically reduced the breeding success of the bird.

The introduction of herbicides had direct consequences for birds that relied on weed seeds for their diet and on insects and other creatures associated with these plants. This then affected birds higher up the food chain that fed on these insects. Consequently, in our unnatural country-side today, it is no wonder that bird numbers have plummeted. Corn bunting, grey partridge, lapwing, skylark and many others have decreased in number at an alarming rate. These birds may not be directly poisoned by toxic chemicals but it is known that toxins can build up and affect a bird's immune system, thus making them more prone to disease and more vulnerable in bad weather.

Peat bogs

During the past century, drainage for agriculture and forestry and the commercial extraction of peat for the horticultural industry have caused a dramatic reduction of the lowland peat bogs in Britain. 'Raised bogs', such as Thorne and Hatfield Moors near Doncaster, are rich in their diversity of plants and wildlife, with over 3,000 different species of insect, more than 800 flowering plants and important fungi, lichens, liverworts and mosses. Peatland birdlife includes many waders and wildfowl, whinchat, merlin, short-eared owl and the nightjar. In Ireland, 17 per cent of the whole land surface was originally peatland. Only about 20 per cent of this area now survives to be of any conservation and scientific importance.

Modern milling methods of peat extraction are still destroying vast areas of this unique habitat and the demand for peat continues to be strong. Gardeners buy all manner of peat products, from seed and cutting composts, growbags and peat pots, to solid bales of peat. Even young plants in the garden centre are, more often than not, grown in peat. To help halt this decline, use a peat alternative in the garden.

Limestone pavements

It has been estimated that as much as 97 per cent of Britain's 2,600 hectares of limestone pavement (which is also known as Westmorland stone or Cumbrian stone) has been damaged or stripped of stone for use by gardeners in rockeries and other landscape features, or by farmers to improve their pasture. Over thousands of years rain water has weathered the limestone into its characteristic pavement-like slabs of rock (clints), with shallow run-off channels (runnels) draining into deep fissures (grikes). It can be found in parts of Cumbria, Lancashire and Yorkshire and in small areas of Scotland and Wales. It supports a special flora of common and rare plants. Hawthorn (*Crataegus*) and bloody cranesbill (*Geranium sanguineum*) can thrive in the deep fissures, even in exposed conditions at high altitudes, and rarer plants such as the rigid buckler fern (*Dryopteris submontana*), brittle bladder fern (*Cystopteris fragilis*), angled Solomon's seal (*Polygonatum odoratum*) and dark red helleborine orchid (*Epipactis atrorubens*) can be found. The birdlife it supports includes the wheatear and the wren, which has the Latin name of *Troglodytes troglodytes*, meaning cave dweller.

To help save this precious landscape from further destruction, avoid using this waterworn limestone for garden rockeries.

PEAT ALTERNATIVES

- **Coir** This is ground-up waste from the coconut industry. Unfertilized blocks can be added to other composts or used as mulch. Fertilized blocks can be used as seed and potting composts. Care must be taken when watering as the compost is like a sponge and in cool conditions young plants and seedlings seem more prone to damp off.

- **Leaf mould** Leaves degenerate slowly into leaf mould. After one year, this mould can be used outside to improve the soil structure, either by digging it in or applying it over the garden borders as surface mulch. After two or more years the finer leaf mould, once sieved, can be used as a peat substitute, seed and potting compost.

- **Garden compost** Used outside to enrich the nutrient content of the soil.

- **Well-rotted cow/chicken/horse manure** Used outside to enrich the soil.

- **Cocoa shell/bark chippings** Used for mulches.

- **Composts and soil improvers** Examples which may be locally available include spent hops (waste from the brewing industry), old mushroom compost, wool shoddy, composted bracken and composted willow bark. Wool shoddy is the shredded waste from the wool industry. Although scarce, these days it can be used as a soil improver; dug into the ground in autumn, it will release nitrogen over a long period of time.

In recent years farming has become increasingly mechanized, leading to the destruction of natural habitats and the loss of hedgerows to make way for cereal crops.

WILDFLOWER LAWNS AND MEADOWS

An open space in a garden is useful for birds and humans alike. Blackbirds, song thrushes and robins will pace up and down the lawn in search of tasty morsels, particularly in damp weather when the earthworms are near the surface. Armies of starlings may descend from rooftops in their hunt for leatherjackets beneath the short swathes of grass. Green woodpecker and, more exotically, a hoopoe may visit a lawn, searching out ants. Longer grass and meadows provide the habitat for a greater diversity of insects and thus encourage other birds, such as the seed-eating finches and sparrows.

Lawns

Not all lawns are bird friendly. Although they are highly prized horticulturally, green velvet swathes are at total odds with nature and are therefore most alien to birds. To keep a lawn in such condition requires much pampering and work, and the fertilizers, weedkillers, and even maybe insecticides used to remove the unwanted chafer bugs and leatherjackets, help to make it a sterile area. In addition, during dry, hot summers, these lawns need copious amounts of water to prevent them becoming parched. Garden sprinklers can use an estimated 17½ pints (10 litres) of water a minute, which is wasteful of this precious resource.

The number of song thrushes is declining, especially in the countryside. Farming practices have reduced its habitat, making gardens increasingly important places for song thrushes to live.

Daisies are low-growing plants found in grassy habitats. They thrive on untreated lawns and can be undamaged by mowing or animals grazing. A wildlife lawn will attract a variety of insects and birds.

The traditional springtime application of either lawn sand or the modern combined lawn feed and weedkiller will eradicate weeds and promote lush green growth. It will also increase the acidity of the soil which, in turn, will discourage worms – one of the gardener's main allies and an important source of food for birds, as shown in the tables on page 146.

Worms are vital in the garden, as they break down organic matter to produce humus, a rich growing medium in which plants thrive. Incredibly, in the past, wormicides were used on lawns to eradicate these valuable creatures as not only are their wormcasts unsightly on well-manicured lawns but they also provide a foothold for weed seeds to germinate. Wormicides are no longer available for use in private gardens.

A new threat to the earthworm populations in Britain is the appearance of flatworms from Australia and New Zealand. These have no natural predators in Britain. If our native worm population crashes due to the spread of these flatworms, the consequences for birds and other native wildlife will be disastrous. If you find a flatworm in the garden, destroy it.

In your own garden, try to create a diverse wildflower lawn. Daisy, clover, bird's-foot trefoil, creeping buttercup, common chickweed, mouse-ear chickweed, germander speedwell (*Veronica chamaedrys*), slender speedwell (*V. filiformis*) and self-heal (*Prunella vulgaris*) are all common low-growing plants that thrive on poor, untreated lawns. (See the table on page 146.) Chamomile (*Anthemis nobilis*) and creeping thyme (*Thymus serpyllum*) can be incorporated amongst the grass. The lawn can be mown weekly during summer, but raise the cutting height to allow some plants to flower and seed or refrain from mowing during the height of the flowering period for a couple of weeks from late May into June.

BIRDWATCHER'S TIP

Feeding the lawn will encourage the grass to grow at the expense of 'weed' species. A weed is only a plant in the wrong place and a 'weedy' lawn is preferable for birdwatchers, as it will attract a greater diversity of insect life which, in turn, means more varied food for birds.

A wildflower lawn does require a little additional maintenance. Some plants are more 'socially' acceptable in a garden than others. For instance, although the seeds of dandelions provide food for finches, it may be wise to prevent them from seeding. A puff of wind is sure to send a snowstorm of those tiny, delicate, floating parachutes over the hedge, much to the angst of the neighbours!

Spring meadows

Other areas of lawn can be left unmown for the first half of the year and planted up with spring bulbs and other native flowers. These will attract early insects into the garden.

By incorporating spring meadow flowers into lawns of low fertility (nitrogenous fertilizers encourage rampant grass growth at the expense of native flowers), such lawns can be nurtured over the years into plant-rich meadows. This method involves planting pot-grown plants into the lawn during late September/October or late March/April and is easier than painstakingly removing the top layer of turf and sowing a seed mixture in spring, though the latter may be essential with highly fertile ground.

In sunny areas, crocus, daffodils, grape hyacinths and tulip bulbs will all thrive, as will the native cowslip *(Primula veris)*, also known as peggles, with its yellow, nodding heads flowering in April and May. In partially shaded areas, bulbs such as snowdrops *(Galanthus)*, wild daffodil *(Narcissus pseudonarcissus)*, bluebell *(Hyacinthoides non-scripta)*, or Spanish bluebell *(H. hispanica)* can be grown between meadow flowers such as primroses *(Primula vulgaris)* and common dog violet *(Viola riviniana)*. In areas of damp soil, snake's-head fritillary *(Fritillaria meleagris)* look effective with cuckoo flower *(Cardamine pratensis)*, whilst ragged robin *(Lychnis flos-cuculi)* flowers slightly later in May and June.

In the south of England, many ancient woodlands have been irreversibly damaged by the commercial stripping of bluebells for the horticultural trade. This has been done to such an extent that the bluebell and many other wildflowers have been given extra protection in law under the Wildlife and Countryside Act of 1981. Meadows should be mown only once the leaves of the bulbs have died back and the flowers have had time to set seed. This will ensure

Flowering bulbs such as daffodils will easily naturalize in lawns and grassy banks.

To create a garden meadow, delay cutting the grass until late summer to enable meadow flowers and grasses to set seed.

a good display of flowers the following year. Crocus and snowdrops may be mown in early May but, generally, wait until late May to June onwards, depending on the plants, then continue mowing the grass every other week until the end of the season.

Summer meadows

Another alternative to a monoculture lawn is to develop the area into a summer meadow or hay meadow, thus providing a seed and insect larder for birds. Cutting the grass should be delayed until late August through to September, depending on the geographical region and the weather. This will enable the meadow flowers and grasses to set seed. Many of these grasses are food plants for the caterpillars of such butterflies as the gatekeeper, meadow brown, ringlet, small skipper and wall. The selection of meadowland flora, including betony (*Stachys officinalis*), common toadflax (*Linaria vulgaris*), devil's bit scabious (*Succisa pratensis*), field scabious (*Knautia arvensis*), knapweed (*Centaurea sp.*), lady's bedstraw (*Galium verum*), lady's mantle (*Alchemilla vulgaris*), meadow buttercup (*Ranunculus acris*), meadow cranesbill (*Geranium pratense*), ox-eye daisy (*Leucanthemum vulgare*), yarrow (*Achillea millefolium*) and yellow rattle (*Rhinanthus minor*), can make it an attractive area of the garden. Many of these plants thrive in different conditions; it may be helpful to look at the rural road verges in your neighbourhood, to see whichplants are best suited to your garden.

BIRDWATCHER'S TIP

Never dig up wild bulbs or plants from the countryside. Only buy cultivated bulbs, plants or seeds from a reputable dealer. This is important as many of our once common native flowers are becoming increasingly scarce in the wild.

PROBLEM WEEDS

Wildflower lawns, spring meadows and summer meadows all need some management, and selective weeding must be undertaken – especially with vigorous rooting plants such as ground elder, Japanese knotweed and horsetails. Dandelion, willowherb and thistle, with their feather-light, downy seed heads that disperse in the breeze, must be controlled. Ragwort can also be a problem weed: although its bright yellow flowers attract many insects, it is poisonous to cattle and therefore should not be allowed to spread.

As an alternative to digging, a weedy area of garden can be cleared by covering the ground with a section of old carpet or plastic sheeting, or a thick layer of newspaper topped with 2–3in (60–80mm) of grass mowings. Without light, the weeds beneath will rot. I have tried the latter on a dense patch of ground elder, leaving the paper and clippings in place for a year, and although it did not quite rot the roots it kept the weed in check, and the soil was friable so it was easy to remove remaining roots by hand.

Meadow flowers and grasses are food for insects, which in turn encourages birds to visit the area.

GARDEN BIRDS THAT WILL FEED ON EARTHWORMS

Kestrel	Mistle thrush
Pheasant	Redwing
Moorhen	Fieldfare
Black-headed gull	Robin
Woodpigeon	Blackcap
Stock dove	Coal tit
Little owl	Jay
Tawny owl	Magpie
Green woodpecker	Jackdaw
Great spotted woodpecker	Rook
Dunnock	Starling
Blackbird	House sparrow
Song thrush	

MAMMALS THAT WILL FEED ON EARTHWORMS

Badger	Hedgehog
Bank vole	House mouse
Common shrew	Mole
Fox	Wood mouse

WILDFLOWERS IN LAWNS

Plant	Flowering time	Description
Bird's-foot trefoil (*Lotus corniculatus*)	May–September	Perennial, with small, orange/yellow, pea-like flowers. A food plant for jackdaw and brambling.
Clover (*Trifolium spp.*)	May–October	Perennial. A food plant for finches, pigeons, rook, crow and yellowhammer.
Common chickweed (*Stellaria media*)	All year	Tiny, white-flowering annual. A food plant for buntings, finches, partridges and pigeons as well as pied wagtail and waxwing.
Creeping buttercup (*Ranunculus repens*)	May–September	Glossy, yellow-flowering perennial. A food plant for many finches, pigeons and other birds.
Daisy (*Bellis perennis*)	All year	Yellow- and white-flowering perennial. A food plant for chaffinch, linnet, redpoll, twite and others.
Mouse-ear (*Cerastium fontanum*)	April–November	Tiny, white-flowering perennial. A food plant for buntings, finches and woodpigeon.
Self-heal (*Prunella vulgaris*)	June–November	Purple-flowering perennial. A food plant for goldfinch and greenfinch, linnet, twite and willow tit.
Speedwells (*Veronica chamaedrys, V. filiformis*)	April–June	Small, blue- and mauve-flowering perennials. Food plants for finches and pigeons.

ENVIRONMENTALLY-FRIENDLY PEST CONTROL

Insects, as mentioned in previous chapters, are an important component of a bird's diet, but in many gardens these same insects are classified as pests. It is common horticultural practice to reach for the appropriate chemical spray, pellet or powder as soon as problems are seen. Not only do these pesticides deprive birds of a potential meal, they may eradicate other beneficial insects such as bees, beetles, hoverflies, lacewings, ladybirds and also spiders, thus damaging the balance of nature in the garden. For example, lacewings, hoverfly larvae, ladybirds and their larvae devour great numbers of aphids. Use a contact pesticide on an aphid infestation and the beneficial insects may be destroyed as well. When pest numbers multiply again, there are no natural predators to keep the pest in check and consequently more pesticide will be needed. With repeated applications, the pest may build up a resistance to the pesticide and a yet more potent chemical will be required for equal effect.

Systemic insecticides are less harmful to other associated insects. These are usually manufactured chemicals, which, when applied, are absorbed by the plant through its leaves or roots. The chemical is then conveyed throughout the plant in its sap, coming into contact only with sap-feeding pests such as aphids. In this way, systemic insecticides are selective, affecting only targeted pests rather than the targeted pests plus other beneficial garden insects. However, reducing the natural abundance of aphids will, in turn, reduce the numbers of its natural predators and hence, reduce the food available for birds.

Lupins are susceptible to aphid infestations during the summer months and although spraying with an insecticide will preserve the aesthetic quality of the plant, it reduces the available food supply for birds. Daily, in late July and August, we have watched blue tits and house sparrows climb the staircase of seed pods and remove the succulent green insects.

In a garden for birds it is best to work with nature, as organically as possible. Use pesticides sparingly, if at all. For pests such as aphids, mealy bugs, red spider mite, thrip and whitefly, try soft soap or an insecticidal soap which loses its potency within a day.

Pyrethrum, although organic in origin, is not selective and is capable of eradicating ants, beetles, wasps and many beneficial insects as well. Pyrethrum is also highly toxic to fish, so must be kept away from water.

A goldfinch feeds mainly on seeds and insects. The use of fertilizers or insecticides in the town or country will impact on a bird's ability to feed.

The slug problem

Song thrushes, once a common bird in gardens, are now in decline. Could a possible factor be the amounts of slug bait used in agriculture and gardens where the poison is often spread indiscriminately over the soil? Slugs and snails form a major part of the diet of thrushes and a large number of mammals, like the badger, hedgehog and mole, relish a slug or two. Lizards, frogs, toads and slow worms also eat slugs and snails. Consequently, using slug bait will affect a large number of creatures.

NON-CHEMICAL SLUG CONTROL

- Introduce nematodes into your garden. Nematodes provide a biological control over slug populations, but they will only be effective for about six weeks, as they have a short life span, and if they are required over large areas of garden, the price becomes prohibitively expensive.
- Arrange cocoa shell mulch around prone plants. This is said to discourage cats as well as slugs, but the resultant population explosion of woodlice may be worse than the effects of slugs.
- Spread coarse grit around prone plants. This helps to deter slugs because they don't like sharp, rough surfaces.
- Cultivate the land or soil regularly. This will bring the slug eggs to the surface, enabling the birds to find them in the soil.
- Set traps for slugs by placing a saucer of beer or milk on the ground near all the attacked plants. These traps will act as a magnet to any nearby slugs.
- Place halved and empty grapefruit or orange skins on the ground. Slugs will seek out the moisture from the peel and can be easily removed every morning.
- Plant your most precious plants, like hostas, in pots with a thick layer of vaseline around the rim: slugs seem not to like contact with the sticky surface.

NB: Slugs are mostly nocturnal creatures and can be picked off plants by torchlight.

Surely, rather than use potent chemicals, a better alternative is to encourage the natural predators of slugs into the garden. Wildlife-friendly slug killers (such as pellets of aluminium sulphate) work by drying out the slug's slime-producing organs, but these are not effective in damp weather, as the concentration of the slug killer is diluted so the slug can recover even though it has been in contact with the bait.

These molluscs are such an important element in the diet of so many birds and mammals (see the tables at the top of page 154), it may be better to direct slugs away from your favourite plants, especially those prone to slug damage like delphiniums, hostas and tulips.

Fruit trees and orchards

The bullfinch is another once-familiar garden bird that is becoming less common in Britain. These birds are traditionally not gardeners' favourites as they have the destructive habit of systematically stripping every blossom flower,

---

GARDEN CHEMICALS CHECK LIST

- Always follow the instructions on the label. Never be tempted to exceed the dosage: it may do more harm than good.
- Apply insecticide on a still, dry day, preferably in the evening when fewer beneficial insects are on the wing.
- To prevent harm to bees and hoverflies, never apply insecticide to flowers.
- Take care when using herbicides and insecticides at ground level. Keep pets from walking over the treated area. Cats especially will invariably sit down and lick their paws having walked over an affected area, thus taking in some of the poison.
- Always wash your hands after using insecticides and herbicides.
- Store chemicals in their original containers, out of the reach of children and pets.

from hud to bud, branch to branch and tree to tree, from every apple, pear, cherry and plum in the orchard. A flock of these birds could spell disaster for the fruit crop. In commercial orchards, and in many gardens, fruit trees are invariably sprayed against aphids, caterpillars, moths, sawflies, weevils and many other pests. As a consequence, bullfinches may be directly affected by these pesticides, and with the resultant loss of insects, many other birds will be deprived of a potential meal.

Some birds are our allies. It has been estimated that about 95 per cent of codling moth eggs in orchard fruit trees are eliminated by roving parties of tits. Many birds come into

Bullfinches were once a major pest of orchards, but since the mid 1970s, there has been a sharp fall in the bird's population.

our garden to feed in the old apple trees, from the colourful great spotted woodpecker to the tiny goldcrest, blue, great and coal tits, nuthatches and treecreepers. Encouraging these birds into the garden will help to keep pest numbers down and keep nature in a healthy balance.

Vegetable patches and allotments

A vegetable patch, whether on an allotment or in a tiny corner of the garden, can be transformed into a bird-friendly area. Over winter, flocks of linnets and goldfinches may descend to the allotments in search of weed seeds.

Smaller insects, such as blackfly and greenfly, also thrive on many crops and in turn provide food for tits, dunnock and wren. For vegetables, as for fruits, it is better to restrict the use of pesticides and adopt environmentally-friendly methods of pest control. These methods include using natural barriers, biological controls, and companion planting. The Henry Doubleday Research Association (Garden Organic) has gardens at Ryton, Warwickshire and Yalding near Maidstone, Kent, and these may be well worth a visit for further ideas on organic gardening (visit www.gardenorganic.org.uk).

Allotments: a patchwork of small gardens can provide food and shelter for birds throughout the year.

TAME ROBIN

IIIIIIIIIIIIIIIIIIIIIIIIIIIIIIIIIIIIIIIIIIIIIIIIIIIIIIIIIIIIIIIIIIIIII

A common sight for many gardeners is a tame robin hopping nearby on newly dug soil and singing a few bars of twittering song close overhead. The process of tilling unearths all sorts of different insects and larvae, with chafer bugs, cutworms and wire-worms, together with slugs' eggs, slugs and earthworms, providing a feast for the robin, blackbird, song thrush and starling.

NON-CHEMICAL METHODS OF PEST CONTROL

- Cover susceptible crops, including brassicas and carrot, with an enviromesh. This fine netting protects the crop from pests such as carrot fly, cabbage-root fly and butterfly caterpillars, and also from pigeons.

- Place brassica collars around the stems of brassica plants. This will deter cabbage-root fly. Cabbage-root flies lay their eggs in the soil next to the stems of young brassica plants. The tiny larvae which hatch from these eggs burrow down to the roots and begin to feed, damaging and, over time, killing the plant. Brassica collars form a barrier that prevents the flies from laying their eggs in the soil.

- Introduce natural predators of the harmful pests. Natural biological controls are less harmful to garden wildlife than chemical controls and are becoming increasingly available to gardeners. Tiny, natural predators include types of nematodes, which feed on slugs or vine weevils (adults and larvae), and Encarsia wasps which feed on whitefly. (Biological controls such as nematodes are available from mail-order suppliers; addresses can be found in gardening magazines.)

- Grow a few flowering plants amongst the vegetables. This will encourage beneficial insects, such as hoverflies whose larvae devour great numbers of aphids. A few bright flowers of candytuft (*Iberis*), *Tagetes*, including French marigolds, nasturtiums (*Tropaeolum*), poached egg plant (*Limnanthes douglasii*), poppies (*Papaver*) and pot marigolds (*Calendula officinalis*) planted with the vegetables will help keep aphid numbers under control. (Further examples of companion plants and their effects can be found in the table at the bottom of page 154.)

- Avoid treated seeds. Some vegetable seeds are treated with a seed dressing of insecticides and fungicides. This is in order to enhance the success of germination, but unfortunately it makes the seeds harmful to all wildlife.

POTENTIAL HAZARDS FOR BIRDS

In any garden there are many potential hazards for birds, a few of which are listed below.

Hedge cutting

Traditionally, hedge cutting is completed in late autumn and early spring before the new season's growth begins. Try to avoid cutting the hedge between March and July, which is the nesting season, and take care either side of these months: there may be an early bird nesting in an unseasonably warm February and some birds may raise late second or third broods. Never expose a nest by clipping – always check the hedge first before you start. An exposed nest is more likely to fail because it will be visible to predators such as the crow, jackdaw and magpie.

Garden netting

This is used to protect crops of soft fruit and vegetables from birds, but it can be hazardous to them. Blackbirds are particularly prone to becoming ensnared in the nets covering strawberries. If you do use netting, check it regularly to ensure that no bird is entangled for long. Never leave bundles of loose netting lying on the ground, particularly around the bases of shrubs, as this is likely to ensnare song thrushes. Stiff-sided fruit cages for soft fruits and a fine mesh fleece for vegetables and strawberry plants may be a worthwhile investment. Otherwise, perhaps the kindest solution in a birdwatcher's garden would be to share the fruit with the birds.

Cotton

Thread is weaved in and out of the branches of fruit trees to keep birds from damaging the flower buds. Having once found a dead robin dangling from one leg on an old piece of thread, we do not encourage this.

Water butts and watering cans

All containers should have their lids in place or be stored on their sides, empty, to reduce the risks they pose to birds and wildlife. Blackbirds have been known to drown in water butts and we once found a tiny dead bank vole inside an upright watering can which was stored away over winter inside our greenhouse.

Buildings

Check outhouses and greenhouses regularly to ensure that no birds have become trapped inside.

Windows

Due to reflections in the glass or to blind panic caused by a pursuing raptor, a bird may fly straight into a window with a loud thud. Such an impact can kill or at least cause concussion. If this happens regularly at a particular window, cut out a black, hawk-shaped silhouette and fix this to the glass; this should help prevent further collisions.

Cats

In recent years cats have become more popular than dogs as pets and thus the pressures on garden bird populations are on the increase. It is important to note that not all cats hunt birds although millions of wild birds are killed each year by these feline predators. Nestlings and fledglings are particularly prone, as they cannot fly out of reach. To discourage cats in the garden:

- avoid growing plants that cats love (catmint, catnip and *Actinidia kolomikta*);
- grow prickly plants such as globe thistles, holly, mahonia and roses, and scatter a few of these leaves on any dry, bare soil to prevent cats basking in the sun;
- place other deterrents, such as chicken wire, orange peel, moth balls and pepper dust, over the garden – they seem not to like the

smell of these last three. Pepper dust is also a deterrent for dogs and rats, and possibly squirrels as well.

Predators

There is a large number of predators of garden songbirds. Even in suburban gardens it is quite common to see sparrowhawk and kestrel and to hear the night-time hootings of a tawny owl. Grey squirrels and rats, carrion crows, magpies and jackdaws will all raid nests; even the great spotted woodpecker and great tit will attack nests when there is a shortage of caterpillars with which to feed their young.

Traffic

Blackbirds are particularly prone to the dangers of cars, as they have a tendency to skim low over the road from one garden to the next. In our garden there is a female blackbird that has become very aware of traffic. She perches on a gate post or the low wall and waits, listening with her head tilted slightly to one side, as though she has learnt the 'green cross code'. When there is a lull she flies safely across to the lawns on the other side to feed. Her offspring are not so

clever. Newly fledged and desperate to follow the food supplier, one youngster flew straight at a passing car, missing it by millimetres. It managed to return to the relative safety of our garden – many other birds are not so fortunate.

DAMAGE BY BIRDS

However attractive, some birds can be very destructive in a garden. Woodpigeons devour peas and cabbage plants at a considerable rate. In our garden one pigeon has taken a fancy to the unripe, hard, green whitecurrants. Sparrows love to luxuriate in dust baths on any newly raked, dry seed beds, but why should they shred yellow primrose and crocus flowers in spring? This is not fully understood. Pheasants in the garden will devour all the daffodil bulbs.

Many birds will eat plastic, putty, mortar and whitewash and will shred foil milk bottle tops to get at the milk inside. (To prevent the spread of disease, ensure that milk bottles are covered.) To really enjoy the birds, you must tolerate their not so pleasant antics.

A woodpigeon feeds on seeds, grains and crops. It can devastate allotment gardens.

If a pheasant comes into a garden, it will eat plant leaves, shoots, seeds, bulbs, berries and beetles, bugs, spiders and worms.

BIRDS THAT WILL FEED ON SLUGS AND SNAILS

Pheasant	Mistle thrush
Moorhen	Redwing
Woodpigeon	Fieldfare
Feral pigeon	Robin
Stock dove	Crow
Tawny owl	Rook
Blackbird	Jackdaw
Song thrush	Starling

BIRDS THAT WILL FEED ON SMALL SNAILS

Wren	Long-tailed tit
Dunnock	Blue tit
Blackcap	Great tit
Chiffchaff	Coal tit
Willow warbler	Nuthatch
Spotted flycatcher	Treecreeper

COMPANION PLANTS

Crop plant	Companion plant	May help deter
Brassicas	Clover	Aphids, cabbage-root fly, small and large white butterfly caterpillars
Brassicas	French beans	Cabbage-root fly, mealy aphids
Brassicas	*Tagetes* (incl. French marigolds)	Whitefly, small and large butterfly caterpillars
Broad beans	Summer savory	Blackfly
Carrots	Leeks, onion, sage	Carrot fly
Onions	Carrot, parsley	Onion fly
Tomatoes	Basil	Aphids and other insects
Tomatoes	*Tagetes* (incl. French marigolds)	Whitefly

RECYCLING

Ideally, every bit of garden waste (weeds, grass mowings, hedge trimmings and prunings) should be recycled, either by composting or by shredding, thereby returning the goodness to the soil. However, there are exceptions: any diseased or badly infested material should be burnt (if bonfires are allowed in your area) or disposed of in an appropriate way.

Bonfires

Bonfires should only be lit in dry conditions when there is a slight breeze blowing away from any houses and roads, as smoke can be a nuisance to neighbours and traffic. Ensure that all the materials are dry, as it is more environmentally friendly to have a quick, hot, less smoky fire than a slow-burning bonfire that lasts for days. In autumn and winter, always check the bonfire heap for any hibernating hedgehogs before lighting.

Leaf piles

In the autumn, rake up leaves to form a pile in a secluded part of the garden. This will become a haven for overwintering insects and worms, and blackbirds and other thrushes will turn the leaves over looking for the tasty morsels. Once the leaves have rotted, the pile will produce a fine leaf mould which, when sieved, can be used either as a substitute compost for peat or as a mulch on garden borders. Mulches suppress weed growth, improve soil structure and reduce the rate of evaporation from the soil – an important consideration following our recent hot summers.

Composting

Soft hedge trimmings, autumn leaves, grass mowings and weeds (but not seeding weeds or the long, fibrous-rooted bindweed and ground elder) can all be composted together with kitchen waste such as eggshell, uncooked fruit and vegetable scraps; meat scraps should not be included as they attract rats and other vermin. Tea and shredded newspaper can also be composted.

A simple compost container can be made by setting four stout wooden posts in a square, about one metre apart, and enclosing the square with chicken wire. Alternatively, compost bins can be purchased in garden centres or by mail order. It will take about a year for compost to rot completely. To speed up the process, build up the sides of the container with wood, leaving ventilation holes in the side. With this increased insulation, the contents of the heap warm up to a high temperature which quickens the process of decomposition. The end result – a dark, crumbly, nutrient-rich humus – can be dug into the soil or spread over borders as a mulch. Ideally, you should have two heaps, one in the process of composting and the other providing a supply of well-rotted compost that is ready for use.

You can enjoy birds visiting your garden all year round. This last chapter, the birdwatcher's year, encapsulates the appearance, behaviour and departure of birds in the garden month by month, throughout the seasons.

The birdwatcher's year

BIRDS THROUGH THE SEASONS

The appearance of birds in gardens is governed by the seasons. For convenience, we have grouped the seasons approximately, into three-monthly periods, following the Garden Birdwatch Scheme of the British Trust for Ornithology. Winter is regarded as the first three months of the year, spring from April to June, summer from July to September and autumn from October to the year's end.

The first signs of spring can arrive early or late, and it is the same for the other seasons. These variations depend on the garden's location and on the weather, so there can be no fixed date for the change of season. Frequently one season just merges into the next.

Winter

January, the beginning of a new year, is an extension of a colder period. If snow lies and conditions are hard, more birds will desperately seek our assistance. The bird table will be in great demand and, depending on the locality, the greater the variety of food supplied, the greater the variety of birds that will visit.

We expect to see various finches, house sparrows, starlings, wrens, dunnocks, thrushes (including robins and blackbirds), collared doves, woodpigeons, jackdaws and, if lucky, one or two blackcaps. Our hanging nuts and sunflower seeds attract more tits, but also attract nuthatches, which disappear when the great spotted woodpecker arrives for the food.

Occasionally a pair of jays will arrive and hunt for any fallen peanuts. Magpies (which we do not encourage) and a juvenile piebald carrion crow also appear. Sometimes a brambling will search for seed. Its search is mainly at ground level, but we have occasionally seen it feeding at the bird table when there is not much competition around. Brambling usually appear in the company of chaffinches, when the local beech mast is exhausted. If the blackbird is elsewhere, a song thrush will fly up to the bird table for scraps. The wren mostly hunts for tiny morsels under the shelter of hedges but does also investigate the bird table. Many of these birds have to wait for jackdaws to depart before they can start feeding.

When apples are thrown out on the ground, redwings and fieldfares join the other thrushes and blackbirds for the feast. In our garden, the appearance of fieldfares and mistle thrushes is only sporadic but a short distance away they are regular visitors. We do, however, see a number of redwings. They spend their time foraging in the leaf litter at the far end of the garden and also consume fallen apples and berries, including snowberry and guelder rose.

(Opposite, top) In winter the mistle thrush will look for fruits and berries, including mistletoe.

(Left) When the ground is frozen in winter, small birds need plenty of help to find food.

BLACKCAP
||||||||||||||||||||||||||||||||||||||||||||||||||||||||||||||

The blackcap feasts on apples and bird table food. Most winters we see both the black-capped male and the quieter, brown-capped female. We have had excellent views of these birds eating apples thrown out near the house. Some male blackcaps appear very aggressive at the bird table, chasing away not only other blackcaps but also sparrows and finches.

Yellowhammers are found in low farmland areas and may visit neighbouring gardens.

When the birches and alders have shed most of their seed, siskins arrive to drink at the pond and eat peanuts. Later in the year their numbers increase; so far the maximum is eight feeding from a couple of peanut holders! Long-tailed tits can be seen using hedges like staircases to reach any food supplies that may be available.

During hard spells in more rural gardens, pheasants will visit bird tables and both marsh and willow tits will be regular visitors. Gardens near fields may be hosts to reed buntings and yellowhammers. One garden near us has had 250 greenfinches and a 100 or more chaffinches with charms of goldfinches. However, in the last year or two, the numbers have been much reduced. The owner of this garden is meticulous, clearing up any waste and droppings at the end of the day in order to prevent rodents and diseases spreading into the area.

In February, the first lesser celandine flowers brighten up any patch that will be subject to dense shade later. For a few days one February, we had 14 first-winter carrion crows in a loose flock in the trees at the bottom of our garden. They strongly objected to the presence of a magpie and the combined noises were dreadful! At this time of year these juveniles sometimes frequent an area; luckily they did not stay too long with us!

Flocks of foraging blue tits will still pass through at this time. A pair of great tits and two pairs of coal tits seem to prefer our food supplies to what is available elsewhere, and stay around. The drinking water bowl and pond are always in great demand.

If February is mild, a few resident birds commence nesting activities. Usually, nest building at this time of the year takes several weeks rather than the few days it takes later in the year. One early starter, the collared dove, appears to never stop breeding. One pair produced a fledgling in December and the next nest was underway by February. Blackbirds are also early nesters. One pair started nest building in February and produced three robust fledglings in March. This is our earliest garden record for young blackbirds. Many other species collect bits of nesting material either to drop them or to commence building. If the weather turns inclement, these attempts are abandoned.

A mild February leads to more frenzied activity in March. Cold spells cause delays, especially in the north, but either suddenly or gradually, gardens become nesting territories or parts of territories for birds, and numerous border clashes between robins and blackbirds occur.

Further south, and at lower altitudes, plant and bird breeding activities are normally further forward compared with those in the north.

Goldfinches are often seen in groups and are
increasingly visiting gardens for food.

The whitethroat is a summer visitor to Britain.

Spring

Quite often in March we have heard a 'hwoit' call from a shrubby area and, being on the lookout for the first arrivals of chiffchaff or willow warbler, have looked for the summer migrant. The willow warbler's alarm call is a drawn-out 'hooet' whilst the chiffchaff's is more monosyllabic. After looking in vain, the call is finally located coming from a chaffinch in the adjacent apple tree. It is usually several days later that the first hesitant songs of the chiffchaff are heard, and not until April that a willow warbler passes through on its way to a breeding site. Several years ago a pair of willow warblers nested in our garden, and the male spent most of the day singing silvery cadences from the top branches of our silver birch. Tree and bush buds start breaking, the insect population increases and the summer visitors return. The blackcap, having wintered on the continent, returns in early April; the indignant 'tac-tac' call and short, clear warble announce its arrival. The wintering blackcaps quietly disappear from their feeding areas and return to Europe.

Overlapping with the summer arrivals in gardens are the bramblings and siskins. Whilst the large flocks will have disappeared by this time, one or two bramblings, the males resplendent in their magnificent breeding plumage, will have a few last feeds at bird seed, sunflower seed, scraps, millet and peanut granules. The siskins spend even more time feeding on peanuts before they disappear, with the male also singing from nearby trees whilst the female is feeding.

We are hoping that whitethroats will return and breed in our bramble patch: a pair used to nest in a nettle clump, but there have been none in the garden since. One June we had a lesser whitethroat marking out its territory for a month to include parts of our garden and those of several neighbours. It was a male and sang unsuccessfully to attract a mate. After this it disappeared and we have not heard or seen one in the vicinity since.

Swallows, declining in number in this area as the volume of traffic, buildings and patios increases and the number of nesting sites is reduced, do not breed here as often as they did but occasionally fly over, busily catching insects. There used to be a large and thriving colony of house martins near us, along with several pairs that nested under a neighbour's roof but both the colony and the other nests have now gone.

Apart from a few early birds, the majority of swifts arrive back here in May when we hear them screaming around the older buildings and see them weaving in and out to catch flying insects. All their food is caught on the wing. In the evenings, when the swift numbers are over 50, sometimes many more, we know that summer is well on the way. Surprisingly, most house martins seem to arrive here after the swifts!

Whilst summer visitors are arriving, the resident birds are busy breeding. A few may have raised young successfully but early nests have a high failure rate due to attacks by predators whilst the foliage is thin, and the highly unpredictable weather, which can result in food shortages, chilling or soaking of youngsters. Interference with the nests also leads to desertion, especially in the early stages of fledging.

In a few suburban gardens in the Chilterns, notable birds are the red kites; up to 18 birds come together for dead mice and carrion, including chicken carcasses which are thrown out for them.

One fine, memorable evening, a male great spotted woodpecker, which had been taking peanuts away to feed its family, turned up with three fledglings. One youngster was more demanding than the others. The adult stuffed all three with peanut fragments whilst they clung to the apple tree branches.

Two days later, one youngster flew down to the pond, hopped to the edge and went in! There was a lot of splashing, so we wondered if it was drowning, but a very bedraggled specimen emerged and hopped uncertainly towards the trellis gate. Here it managed to flap upwards onto a low bar, shortly to depart.

During June, in a Scottish garden, a blackbird was seen demolishing unripe green Mahonia berries. Greenfinches chew our *Daphne mezereum* berries when unripe, to extract the seeds from the fleshy parts, unlike the blackbird, which was swallowing the whole berries.

Summer

During summer, birds can hide in the thick foliage and nests become difficult to find. Young birds, which can be heard squeaking in the vegetation, are fed on the plentiful insects.

One July afternoon, a baby goldcrest was found amongst the flower pots and boxes at the far end of the greenhouse, away from the door. It was newly fledged from a nest in our neighbour's tall *Chamaecyparis*. We had some difficulty extracting the youngster from the pots, but it was no good leaving it there. Eventually we managed to extract the small bundle and take it to the open door. Suddenly it flew off and landed in a nearby hedge. After a few squeaks, the male parent was seen to fly down and feed the youngster, then they both left to join the rest of the family. Except in a dire emergency such as this, young birds should be left alone, leaving their parents to find and care for them.

By July, our young woodpeckers were independent. One of them became addicted to peanuts, eating them most of the day. We decided to reduce the quantity of peanuts available, to encourage it to spend more time looking for natural foods. This tactic worked and gradually the juvenile, with its red crown, spent less time eating peanuts.

During moult, other birds also forage elsewhere and it is possible, depending on the year, to give up most of the supplementary feeding for a short time, making sure that the essential water is there. The birds themselves indicate if they need the extra food.

This year, for the first time in 30 years, our purple-leaved plum, *Prunus cerasifera* var. atropurpurea, had a few fruits. In other years, the opening flower buds have been stripped systematically by bullfinches in the early spring. This year there were no bullfinches and the house sparrows only destroyed a few flowers.

Some summer migrants start departing in July and August. At some time, after mid-July and before mid-August, there will no longer be large numbers of wheeling swifts, though a few individuals may stay around into September. Swallows and house martins often congregate near nest sites and then depart in waves. The majority disappear by the end of August or mid-September but there are individuals still about in October, usually those with a late second or third brood that still requires feeding.

The resident blackbirds and all their neighbours descend on the ripening berries of rowan, currants, raspberries and strawberries in our garden. This fruit attracts passage migrants and one song thrush has taken up permanent residence in an old redcurrant bush. The whitecurrants used to be disregarded until other fruits had disappeared, but now woodpigeons and blackbirds have discovered that they are very palatable, and devour them while still green. Our raspberries and strawberries are always preferred to our gooseberries. Chokeberries, large, black and shiny, were eaten one year by blackbirds but the next they were disregarded and the gooseberries were preferred!

Passage migrants, if they are not eating seeds or fruits, will feast on insects. Young willow warblers and chiffchaffs regularly hunt for insect food under our shrub and tree leaves. On rare occasions a spotted flycatcher will remain for a few days, catching flies from the apple trees.

In autumn, large numbers of goldcrest migrants arrive in Britain.

Autumn

September merges into October, with fewer summer visitors around. Gardens near the coast are likely to have more unusual visitors, such as a barred warbler eating elderberries in an east coast garden. Even in London, surprise visitors appear in gardens and parks, including British and Scandinavian birds working their way south for the winter, like both redstart species.

Often there is an influx of Scandinavian goldcrests, hunting for insects on conifers and even on our brooms. Other small warblers may also appear. A garden in North Wales missed having a Pallas' warbler by less than 300ft (90m)! The garden owners had excellent views of the crowds that came to observe this small migrant. The rare, tiny, yellow-browed warbler may appear in east- and south-coast gardens, where it can be seen hunting for insects on sycamore leaves.

There is often an overlap between the departure of summering birds and the arrival of winter migrants. This may be more pronounced in the north and at the coast. Swallows still hawk for insects and the first group of redwings circles overhead. By October, autumn is really underway. If it is wet, the trees remain green until November or until the first frosts, when leaf fall occurs. These variations in weather are reflected in bird behaviour. In muggy weather, when there is food in abundance, summer migrants will linger a little longer. With some species, like the chiffchaff, a few individuals do not migrate but overwinter with the aid of a few choice fruits and bird table food to supplement the insects.

The numbers of house sparrows waiting to bathe increases, along with blackbird and starling. We used to have contingents of starlings searching for leatherjackets on our lawn, but they are now scarce.

Tits commence flocking, with groups of up to 100 birds or more. These groups are mainly blue tits, but they also include some coal and great tits. Amalgamated families of long-tailed tits pass through the garden, some taking an interest in the peanut feeder. We once had nine of them all crowded together on a small wire holder. It looked as if the feeder was completely covered in fluffy feathers with long tails sticking outwards!

Long-tailed tits feeding in winter.

With moulting completed and the weather cooler, more birds return to gardens, searching for supplementary food. The nuthatches look for sunflower seeds and peanuts.

If the end of October/beginning of November is warm and damp, five or six black-headed gulls gather and circle over the oak trees bordering the bottom of our garden. Suddenly a gull will swoop down above the tree tops to catch flying insects, then swerve up again for another dive. One or two birds actually land momentarily on the uppermost branches of the trees to collect the gall wasps, newly emerged from the small spangles. (These spangles are small galls found on the lower leaf surfaces of oaks.) This dive bombing ceases after a few days.

The number of finches builds up and other birds, even grey wagtails, will visit gardens for crumbs if the weather is hard. Although we rarely see a rook after food in our garden, several rooks used to visit a small balcony garden for bread.

In an invasion year, waxwings may appear in eastern and northern Britain from November. In this district, they seem to have a gathering place and observation point at the top of a small group of poplars situated in the river valley on the outskirts of the city. This may well also be their arrival place! From these poplars, groups or small flocks fly out at intervals in various directions. A small group will descend on the whitebeam and rowan berries nearby and hang almost upside down or stretch right out to reach the succulent fruit, whilst those still in the poplars may be singing or observing. Other small groups may join them whilst yet more may decide to fly further away in search of food; one group of about 60 birds descended on a lane and the gardens next to it about 2 miles (3½km) away. When the area is denuded of suitable food, the flocks disappear elsewhere. If our garden still contains uneaten

Waxwings on poplars.

berries, these birds can descend and eat the lot. By this stage, nearly all our rowan berries have already been eaten by blackbirds, but we hope that the waxwings might discover our guelder rose berries.

If snow arrives before the end of the year, bramblings come into the garden with the chaffinches and siskins to investigate the peanuts. Frequently, large flocks of both siskins and bramblings fly overhead. Sometimes the siskin flocks are joined by redpolls hunting for food from the birch and alder catkins. One siskin was seen to leave her group feeding in a silver birch and descend to a *Rosa rugosa* hedge where she busily attacked a large hip for its seeds.

By the end of the year the patterns change and scavengers, including flocks of jackdaws, fly around the neighbourhood to see what

is available. Predators also spend more time hunting around gardens. The early strains of the Christmas rose (*Helleborus niger*) together with a sprinkling of other flowers, show that the end of the year has arrived.

Next year there will be differences and surprises in bird numbers and behaviour, and maybe different species. Perhaps even a rarity may suddenly take a liking to the garden's produce!

Hopefully, as increasing numbers of gardens throughout the country become more suited to various birds' requirements, they will help to halt the decline of some of our species which, at present, are at risk; perhaps more gardens will act as oases in desert-like locations.

The waxwing comes to Britain in winter and feeds on hips, haws and rowan berries.

APPENDIX

The list below is divided into two main bird species groups - passerines (also known as passeriformes) or 'perching birds', and non-passerines, being all others. Species are then grouped according to their species families.

Non–passerines
Little grebe *Tachybaptus ruficollis*
Grey heron *Ardea cinerea*
Mute swan *Cygnus olor*
Greylag goose *Anser anser*
Canada goose *Branta canadensis*
Mallard *Anas platyrhynchos*
Tufted duck *Aythya fuligula*
Red kite *Milvus milvus*
Sparrowhawk *Accipiter nisus*
Osprey *Pandion haliaetus*
Kestrel *Falco tinnunculus*
Merlin *Falco columbarius*
Peregrine *Falco peregrinus*
Red-legged partridge *Alectoris rufa*
Partridge (grey) *Perdix perdix*
Pheasant *Phasianus colchicus*
Water rail *Rallus aquaticus*
Corncrake *Crex crex*
Moorhen *Gallinula chloropus*
American purple gallinule *Porphyrula martinica*
Coot *Fulica atra*
Oystercatcher *Haematopus ostralegus*
Lapwing *Vanellus vanellus*
Snipe *Gallinago gallinago*
Redshank *Tringa totanus*
Greenshank *Tringa nebularia*
Common sandpiper *Actitis hypoleucos*
Black-headed gull *Larus ridibundus*
Common gull *Larus canus*
Lesser black-backed gull *Larus fuscus*
Herring gull *Larus argentatus*
Great black-backed gull *Larus marinus*

Feral pigeon *Columba livia*
Stock dove *Columba oenas*
Woodpigeon *Columba palumbus*
Collared dove *Streptopelia decaocto*
Turtle dove *Streptopelia turtur*
Passenger pigeon *Ectopistes migratorius**
 * Extinct since 1914
Ring-necked parakeet *Psittacula krameri*
Cuckoo *Cuculus canorus*
Barn owl *Tyto alba*
Little owl *Athene noctua*
Tawny owl *Strix aluco*
Short-eared owl *Asio flammeus*
Nightjar *Caprimulgus europaeus*
Swift *Apus apus*
Kingfisher *Alcedo atthis*
Bee-eater *Merops apiaster*
Roller *Coracias garrulus*
Hoopoe *Upupa epops*
Green woodpecker *Picus viridis*
Great spotted woodpecker *Dendrocopos major*
Lesser spotted woodpecker *Dendrocopos minor*

Passerines
Skylark *Alauda arvensis*
Sand martin *Riparia riparia*
Swallow *Hirundo rustica*
House martin *Delichon urbica*
Meadow pipit *Anthus pratensis*
Grey wagtail *Motacilla cinerea*
Pied wagtail *Motacilla alba*
Waxwing *Bombycilla garrulus*
Dipper *Cinclus cinclus*
Wren *Troglodytes troglodytes*
Dunnock *Prunella modularis*
Robin *Erithacus rubecula*
Nightingale *Luscinia megarhynchos*
Black redstart *Phoenicurus ochruros*
Common redstart *Phoenicurus phoenicurus*
Whinchat *Saxicola rubetra*
Stonechat *Saxicola torquata*

Wheatear *Oenanthe oenanthe*
Ring ouzel *Turdus torquatus*
Blackbird *Turdus merula*
Fieldfare *Turdus pilaris*
Song thrush *Turdus philomelos*
Redwing *Turdus iliacus*
Mistle thrush *Turdus viscivorus*
Sedge warbler *Acrocephalus schoenobaenus*
Icterine warbler *Hippolais icterina*
Dartford warbler *Sylvia undata*
Barred warbler *Sylvia nisoria*
Lesser whitethroat *Sylvia curruca*
Whitethroat *Sylvia communis*
Garden warbler *Sylvia borin*
Blackcap *Sylvia atricapilla*
Pallas's warbler *Phylloscopus proregulus*
Yellow-browed warbler *Phylloscopus inornatus*
Wood warbler *Phylloscopus sibilatrix*
Chiffchaff *Phylloscopus collybita*
Willow warbler *Phylloscopus trochilus*
Goldcrest *Regulus regulus*
Firecrest *Regulus ignicapillus*
Spotted flycatcher *Muscicapa striata*
Pied flycatcher *Ficedula hypoleuca*
Long-tailed tit *Aegithalos caudatus*
Marsh tit *Parus palustris*
Willow tit *Parus montanus*
Crested tit *Parus cristatus*
Coal tit *Parus ater*
Blue tit *Parus caeruleus*
Great tit *Parus major*
Nuthatch *Sitta europaea*
Treecreeper *Certhia familiaris*
Golden oriole *Oriolus oriolus*
Red-backed shrike *Lanius collurio*
Jay *Garrulus glandarius*
Magpie *Pica pica*
Jackdaw *Corvus monedula*
Rook *Corvus frugilegus*
Carrion crow/Hooded crow *Corvus corone*
Starling *Sturnus vulgaris*

Rose-coloured starling *Sturnus roseus*
House sparrow *Passer domesticus*
Spanish sparrow *Passer hispaniolensis*
Tree sparrow *Passer montanus*
Chaffinch *Fringilla coelebs*
Brambling *Fringilla montifringilla*
Serin *Serinus serinus*
Canary *Serinus canaria*
Greenfinch *Carduelis chloris*
Goldfinch *Carduelis carduelis*
Siskin *Carduelis spinus*
Linnet *Carduelis cannabina*
Twite *Carduelis flavirostris*
Redpoll *Carduelis flammea*
Crossbill *Loxia curvirostra*
Scottish crossbill *Loxia scotica*
Scarlet (common) rosefinch *Carpodacus erythrinus*
Bullfinch *Pyrrhula pyrrhula*
Hawfinch *Coccothraustes coccothraustes*
Dark-eyed junco *Junco hyemalis*
Yellowhammer *Emberiza citrinella*
Cirl bunting *Emberiza cirlus*
Reed bunting *Emberiza schoeniclus*
Corn bunting *Miliaria calandra*

SOURCES OF INFORMATION
Selected bibliography

Bird identification guides
Cramp S, 1977–1994, *The Handbook of Birds of Europe, the Middle East & North Africa*, 9 vols, Oxford University Press

Snow D W & Perrins C M, 1998, *The Birds of the Western Palearctic*, Concise Ed., 2 vols, Oxford University Press

Jonsson L, 1992, *Birds of Europe with North Africa and the Middle East*, Helm

Svensson L, Mullarney K, Zetterström D, Grant P J, 2010, *Collins Bird Guide*, 2nd Ed., Collins

Plant identification guides
Brickell C, 1992, *The Royal Horticultural Society Encyclopedia of Gardening*, Dorling Kindersley

Brickell C, 1995, *The Royal Horticultural Society Gardeners' Encyclopedia of Plants & Flowers*, Dorling Kindersley

Clapham A R, Tutin T G & Warburg E F, 1952, *Flora of the British Isles*, Cambridge University Press

Fitter R, Fitter A & Blamey M, 1984, *The Wild Flowers of Britain and Northern Europe*, Collins

Fitter R & Fitter A, 1984, *Guide to the Grasses, Sedges, Rushes and Ferns of Britain & Northern Europe*, Collins

Mitchell A, 1979, *A Field Guide to the Trees of Britain and Northern Europe*, Collins

Phillips R & Rix M, 1994, *Shrubs*, Garden Plant series, Macmillan

Further bird books
du Feu L, 1993, *Nest Boxes*, 2nd Ed., Guide No. 23, British Trust for Ornithology

Glue D, 1982, *The Garden Bird Book*, Macmillan, British Trust for Ornithology

Mackenzie D, 1997, *Bird Boxes and Feeders for the Garden*, GMC Publications Ltd

Moss S, 2006, *The Garden Bird Handbook: How to Attract, Identify and Watch the Birds in Your Garden*, New Holland

Newton I, 1972, *Finches*, Collins

Perrins C M, 1979, *British Tits*, Collins

Simms E, 1975, *Birds of Town and Suburb*, Collins

Simms E, 1978, *British Thrushes*, Collins

Soper T, 1992, *The Bird Table Book*, 6th Ed., David & Charles

Snow D W, 1958, *A Study of Blackbirds* (reprint 1988 British Museum/Natural History), Allen & Unwin

Snow B & Snow D, 1988, *Birds and Berries*, T & A D Poyser

Witherby H F et al., 1938-1941, *The Handbook of British Birds*, 5 vols, Witherby

General
Baines C, 1984, *How to Make a Wildlife Garden*, Elm Tree Books

Barker G, 1997, *A Framework for the Future: green networks with multiple uses in and around towns and cities*, No. 256, Res Rep, English Nature

Beebee T, 1992, *Pond Life*, Whittet

Chinery M, 1993, *Insects of Britain & Western Europe*, Collins Pocket Guide, Domino

Gilbert O L, 1989, *The Ecology of Urban Habitats*, Chapman & Hall

Hamilton G Ed., 1995, *Organic Gardening*, Pocket Encyclopedia, Dorling Kindersley

Hansson L, 1992, *Ecological Principles of Nature Conservation*, Elsevier

Rackham O, 1986, *The History of the Countryside* (Paperback 1957, Phoenix), J M Dent

Tait M, 2010, *Birds in Your Garden*, RHS/A&C Black

Various County Bird Reports

Various County Flora Reports

Periodicals

BTO News and Bird Study, BTO

RSPB *Birds* magazine

British Birds

Birdwatch and *Birdwatching* magazines

Gardeners' World, *Amateur Gardening* and *Organic Gardening* magazines

Natural World, Wildlife Trusts

Websites

See websites below, plus:
www.naturalengland.org.uk
www.mammal.org.

USEFUL ADDRESSES

General

British Trust for Ornithology (BTO)
The Nunnery
Thetford
Norfolk IP24 2PU
www.bto.org

Royal Society for the Protection of Birds (RSPB)
The Lodge
Sandy
Bedfordshire SG19 2DL
www.rspb.org.uk

The Wildlife Trusts
The Kiln, Waterside
Mathr Road
Newark
Nottinghamshire NG24 1WT
www.wildlifetrusts.org

Royal Horticultural Society (RHS)
80 Vincent Square
London SW1P 2PE
www.rhs.org.uk

Bird food suppliers

Gardman Ltd (customer services)
High Street
Moulton, Spalding
Lincolnshire PE12 6QD
www.gardman.co.uk

Seed suppliers

DT Brown & Co Ltd
Bury Road
Newmarket
Cambridgeshire CB8 7PQ
dtbrownseeds.co.uk

Suttons Consumer Products Ltd
Woodview Road
Paignton
Devon TQ4 7NG
www.suttons.co.uk

Unwins Seeds Ltd
Impington Lane
Histon
Cambridge CB4 9LE
www.unwins.co.uk

ABOUT THE AUTHORS

Hazel and Pamela Johnson have a long-shared interest in wildlife, conservation and ecology which they have followed in their everyday lives and studies.

Hazel has a PhD in geology and has taught botany and geology at universities. She has also been a voluntary group leader for an RSPB local members' group for 20 years, for which she received a President's award. Pamela has completed a course in horticulture. Both have participated in various voluntary bird and wildlife surveys as well as enjoying all aspects of gardening and the countryside.

ACKNOWLEDGEMENTS

Firstly, we thank Steve Young for all his care taken over providing the excellent bird photographs required for this book. Also, we should like to thank: the BTO staff for their helpful suggestions; English Nature, especially Diane Crozier; the RSPB staff, especially T Cleeves and D Hirst; the local Durham RSPB members' group, especially B Howarth and H Wynn; the Durham Wildlife Trust; and the Northern Horticultural Society.

Many others assisted in providing information for this book, including P Gumbley, V Jones, G Laker, O and J Rees, J and A Shore and L Thompson. To all, including those not mentioned by name. we extend our most grateful thanks.

PICTURE CREDITS

INDEX

GMC Publications Ltd, 166 High Street, Lewes, East Sussex, BN7 1XU, United Kingdom

Tel: +44 (0)1273 488005 Fax: +44 (0)1273 402866

www.gmcbooks.com

Contact us for a complete catalogue, or visit our website.